Diabetic Cookb for Beginners

2000 Days of Easy & Delicious Recipes with Healthy Ingredients to Lower Your Blood Sugar for Type 2 Diabetes and Prediabetes

NATHAN TERRELL

TABLE OF CONTENTS

Introduction

Welcome to the "Type 2 Diabetes Cookbook for Beginners"! This cookbook is designed to be your guide to delicious and nutritious eating while managing type 2 diabetes. Whether you are newly diagnosed or have been living with diabetes for some time, this book aims to empower you with the knowledge and tools you need to make healthy choices and take control of your health.

Living with type 2 diabetes can present challenges, but it's important to remember that with the right approach, you can still enjoy a fulfilling and satisfying lifestyle. This cookbook is here to show you that managing your diabetes doesn't mean sacrificing flavor or variety in your meals. Instead, it's about making informed decisions about the foods you eat and adopting habits that support your overall well-being.

In the following pages, you will find a wealth of information on understanding type 2 diabetes, managing your condition effectively, and incorporating delicious, diabetes-friendly recipes into your meal plans. From hearty breakfasts to satisfying dinners, from wholesome snacks to decadent desserts, we have curated a collection of recipes that are not only delicious but also tailored to help you keep your blood sugar levels in check.

But this book is more than just a collection of recipes. It's a comprehensive resource that covers everything from the basics of type 2 diabetes to lifestyle management strategies that can make a real difference in your health. We delve into topics such as the role of medications and insulin therapy, the importance of regular exercise, stress management techniques, and the connection between sleep and diabetes management.

Our goal is to empower you to make positive changes in your life that will support your journey toward better health and well-being. Whether you're looking for practical tips on meal planning, guidance on creating an exercise routine, or inspiration for preparing delicious and nutritious meals, you'll find it all within these pages.

So, let's embark on this journey together. Let's explore the wonderful world of diabetes-friendly cooking and discover how simple, flavorful, and satisfying eating well with type 2 diabetes can be. With the right knowledge, support, and delicious recipes at your fingertips, managing your diabetes can become not just a necessity, but a rewarding and enjoyable part of your everyday life.

Here's to your health and happiness!

Warm regards,

Nathan Terrell

Chapter 1: Understanding Type 2 Diabetes

Type 2 diabetes mellitus is a complex metabolic disorder characterized by chronic hyperglycemia (high blood sugar levels) resulting from insulin resistance and relative insulin deficiency. In this detailed exploration of type 2 diabetes, we will delve into its multifaceted nature, including its pathophysiology, risk factors, epidemiology, clinical presentation, diagnostic criteria, and complications.

1.1 Pathophysiology of Type 2 Diabetes

Type 2 diabetes develops when the body becomes resistant to the actions of insulin or when the pancreas fails to produce enough insulin to meet the body's demands. Insulin resistance occurs primarily in muscle, liver, and adipose tissue cells, leading to impaired glucose uptake and utilization. The beta cells of the pancreas respond by producing more insulin, but over time, this compensatory mechanism may fail, resulting in relative insulin deficiency.

Several mechanisms contribute to insulin resistance, including chronic inflammation, oxidative stress, dysregulated adipokine secretion, mitochondrial dysfunction, and genetic predisposition. Excess adiposity, particularly visceral adipose tissue, plays a central role in the development of insulin resistance through the release of pro-inflammatory cytokines and adipokines.

1.2 Risk Factors for Type 2 Diabetes

Numerous risk factors increase the likelihood of developing type 2 diabetes. These include:

- **Obesity:** Excess adiposity, especially visceral fat accumulation, is strongly associated with insulin resistance and type 2 diabetes.

- **Sedentary Lifestyle:** Physical inactivity contributes to obesity and insulin resistance, making regular exercise an essential component of diabetes prevention and management.

- **Unhealthy Diet:** Diets high in refined carbohydrates, saturated fats, and processed foods increase the risk of obesity and type 2 diabetes.

- **Genetic Predisposition:** Family history and genetic factors significantly influence the risk of type 2 diabetes.

- **Ethnicity:** Certain ethnic groups, including African Americans, Hispanic/Latino Americans, Native Americans, Asian Americans, and Pacific Islanders, are at higher risk.

- **Age:** The risk of type 2 diabetes increases with age, particularly after age 45.

1.3 Epidemiology of Type 2 Diabetes

Type 2 diabetes is a global health concern, with prevalence rates rising dramatically in recent decades. The epidemic of obesity, sedentary lifestyle, and unhealthy dietary habits has fueled the increase in type 2 diabetes prevalence worldwide. According to the International Diabetes Federation (IDF), approximately 463 million adults aged 20-79 years were living with diabetes in 2019, with type 2 diabetes accounting for the vast majority of cases.

1.4 Clinical Presentation and Symptoms

The clinical presentation of type 2 diabetes varies widely and may include:

- **Polyuria:** Excessive urination due to osmotic diuresis resulting from hyperglycemia.

- **Polydipsia:** Increased thirst secondary to dehydration caused by polyuria.

- **Polyphagia:** Excessive hunger due to cellular starvation despite elevated blood glucose levels.

- **Fatigue:** Reduced cellular energy production and utilization due to impaired glucose uptake.

- **Blurred Vision:** Changes in lens osmolarity and refractive index due to hyperglycemia may cause visual disturbances.

However, many individuals with type 2 diabetes remain asymptomatic for years, highlighting the importance of routine screening and early detection.

1.5 Diagnostic Criteria

The diagnosis of type 2 diabetes is based on various criteria established by medical organizations, including the American Diabetes Association (ADA) and the World Health Organization (WHO). Diagnostic tests include fasting plasma glucose (FPG), oral glucose tolerance test (OGTT), and hemoglobin A1c (HbA1c) levels.

1.6 Complications of Type 2 Diabetes

Untreated or poorly managed type 2 diabetes can lead to a myriad of acute and chronic complications, including:

- **Cardiovascular Complications:** Increased risk of coronary artery disease, myocardial infarction, stroke, and peripheral vascular disease.

- **Microvascular Complications:** Retinopathy, nephropathy, and neuropathy can result in vision loss, kidney failure, and peripheral neuropathy.

- **Macrovascular Complications:** Atherosclerosis, hypertension, and dyslipidemia contribute to the development of cardiovascular disease.

- **Infections and Wound Healing:** Impaired immune function and delayed wound healing increase susceptibility to infections and foot ulcers.

Chapter 2: Managing Type 2 Diabetes

Effective management of type 2 diabetes is essential for maintaining optimal health, preventing complications, and improving quality of life. In this comprehensive chapter, we will explore various strategies and interventions aimed at controlling blood sugar levels, promoting overall well-being, and reducing the risk of diabetes-related complications.

2.1 Medications and Insulin Therapy

For many individuals with type 2 diabetes, lifestyle modifications alone may not be sufficient to achieve optimal glycemic control. Pharmacotherapy plays a crucial role in managing blood sugar levels and preventing complications. Several classes of medications are commonly used to treat type 2 diabetes, including:

- **Metformin:** Considered first-line therapy for type 2 diabetes, metformin improves insulin sensitivity, reduces hepatic glucose production, and enhances glucose uptake by peripheral tissues.

- **Sulfonylureas:** These medications stimulate insulin secretion from pancreatic beta cells and can be used as adjunctive therapy to metformin or as monotherapy in certain cases.

- **Dipeptidyl Peptidase-4 (DPP-4) Inhibitors:** DPP-4 inhibitors enhance insulin secretion and reduce glucagon levels, leading to improved glycemic control.

- **SGLT2 Inhibitors:** Sodium-glucose cotransporter 2 (SGLT2) inhibitors reduce renal glucose reabsorption, leading to glycosuria and improved blood sugar control.

- **GLP-1 Receptor Agonists:** Glucagon-like peptide-1 (GLP-1) receptor agonists stimulate insulin secretion, suppress glucagon release, slow gastric emptying, and promote weight loss.

In cases where oral medications are insufficient to control blood sugar levels, insulin therapy may be initiated. Insulin therapy aims to mimic the physiological insulin secretion pattern and may involve the use of basal insulin, bolus insulin, or a combination of both to achieve glycemic targets.

2.2 Blood Sugar Monitoring

Regular blood sugar monitoring is essential for individuals with type 2 diabetes to assess the effectiveness of treatment, identify patterns of hyperglycemia or hypoglycemia, and make informed adjustments to medication regimens and lifestyle habits. Continuous glucose monitoring (CGM) systems provide real-time glucose readings and can help individuals make timely interventions to maintain optimal blood sugar control.

2.3 Healthy Lifestyle Changes

Lifestyle modifications are the cornerstone of type 2 diabetes management and can significantly impact glycemic control and overall health. Key lifestyle changes include:

- **Healthy Eating:** Adopting a balanced diet rich in fruits, vegetables, whole grains, lean proteins, and healthy fats can help regulate blood sugar levels, promote weight loss, and reduce the risk of cardiovascular complications.

- **Regular Physical Activity:** Engaging in regular exercise, such as brisk walking, cycling, swimming, or strength training, improves insulin sensitivity, lowers blood sugar levels, and enhances cardiovascular health.

- **Weight Management:** Achieving and maintaining a healthy weight through calorie control, portion management, and regular physical activity can reduce insulin resistance and improve glycemic control.

- **Smoking Cessation:** Quitting smoking is crucial for individuals with type 2 diabetes, as smoking increases the risk of cardiovascular disease and other complications.

2.4 Importance of Diet and Nutrition

Dietary choices play a pivotal role in managing type 2 diabetes and can significantly impact blood sugar levels, weight management, and overall health. A diabetes-friendly diet should focus on:

- **Carbohydrate Management:** Monitoring carbohydrate intake, choosing complex carbohydrates over simple sugars, and spacing carbohydrate consumption throughout the day can help stabilize blood sugar levels.

- **Portion Control:** Controlling portion sizes and eating regular, balanced meals can prevent blood sugar spikes and promote satiety.

- **Nutrient Density:** Emphasizing nutrient-dense foods, such as fruits, vegetables, whole grains, lean proteins, and healthy fats, provides essential vitamins, minerals, and antioxidants while minimizing empty calories.

Chapter 3: Exercise and Physical Activity

Exercise and physical activity are integral components of a comprehensive approach to managing type 2 diabetes. In this expanded chapter, we will delve into the numerous benefits of exercise, types of physical activity suitable for individuals with diabetes, guidelines for establishing an exercise routine, and strategies for overcoming common barriers to physical activity.

3.1 Benefits of Exercise for Diabetes Management

Regular exercise offers a myriad of benefits for individuals with type 2 diabetes, including:

- **Improved Insulin Sensitivity:** Exercise enhances the body's ability to utilize insulin, leading to better blood sugar control and reduced insulin resistance.

- **Blood Sugar Regulation:** Physical activity helps lower blood sugar levels by increasing glucose uptake by muscle cells and improving insulin sensitivity.

- **Weight Management:** Exercise promotes weight loss and maintenance by burning calories, increasing metabolism, and preserving lean muscle mass.

- **Cardiovascular Health:** Aerobic exercise strengthens the heart, improves circulation, lowers blood pressure, and reduces the risk of cardiovascular complications associated with diabetes.

- **Stress Reduction:** Physical activity releases endorphins, neurotransmitters that promote feelings of well-being and reduce stress, anxiety, and depression.

- **Improved Lipid Profile:** Regular exercise can raise HDL cholesterol (the "good" cholesterol) levels, lower LDL cholesterol (the "bad" cholesterol) levels, and reduce triglyceride levels, improving overall lipid profile.

3.2 Types of Exercise for Diabetes

Various types of exercise can benefit individuals with type 2 diabetes, including:

- **Aerobic Exercise:** Activities such as brisk walking, jogging, cycling, swimming, dancing, and aerobic classes improve cardiovascular fitness, burn calories, and enhance blood sugar control.

- **Strength Training:** Resistance training exercises using weights, resistance bands, or body weight resistance help build muscle mass, increase metabolism, and improve insulin sensitivity.

- **Flexibility and Balance Exercises:** Stretching, yoga, tai chi, and Pilates improve flexibility, balance, coordination, and range of motion, reducing the risk of falls and injuries.

3.3 Creating an Exercise Routine

Establishing a regular exercise routine is key to reaping the benefits of physical activity. Consider the following tips when developing an exercise plan:

- **Set Realistic Goals:** Start with achievable goals and gradually increase the duration, intensity, and frequency of exercise over time.

- **Choose Activities You Enjoy:** Select activities that you enjoy and that fit your lifestyle, preferences, and fitness level to increase adherence and sustainability.

- **Incorporate Variety:** Mix different types of exercise to prevent boredom, avoid overuse injuries, and target different muscle groups.

- **Schedule Regular Workouts:** Set aside dedicated time for exercise on most days of the week, aiming for at least 150 minutes of moderate-intensity aerobic exercise or 75 minutes of vigorous-intensity aerobic exercise per week, along with two or more days of strength training.

3.4 Overcoming Barriers to Physical Activity

Common barriers to physical activity include lack of time, motivation, social support, and access to facilities. Strategies for overcoming these barriers include:

- **Prioritize Exercise:** Make physical activity a priority by scheduling it into your daily routine and treating it as an essential component of diabetes management.

- **Start Slowly:** Begin with low-intensity activities and gradually increase the duration and intensity as your fitness level improves.

- **Find Support:** Seek support from friends, family members, or support groups to stay motivated, accountable, and engaged in regular exercise.

- **Be Flexible:** Be flexible and adaptable in your approach to exercise, modifying activities as needed to accommodate changes in schedule, weather, or physical health.

Chapter 4: Stress Management and Mental Well-Being

Stress management and prioritizing mental well-being are essential aspects of living with and managing type 2 diabetes. In this comprehensive chapter, we explore the profound impact of stress on diabetes management, the connection between stress and blood sugar levels, and strategies for promoting mental health and resilience.

4.1 Understanding the Connection Between Stress and Diabetes

Stress, whether physical or emotional, can have significant implications for individuals with type 2 diabetes. The body's response to stress involves the release of hormones such as cortisol and adrenaline, which can cause blood sugar levels to rise. For individuals with diabetes, this can pose challenges in blood sugar management and increase the risk of hyperglycemia.

Chronic stress can also contribute to unhealthy coping mechanisms such as emotional eating, poor sleep habits, sedentary behavior, and neglect of self-care practices, all of which can further exacerbate diabetes management challenges.

4.2 Techniques for Managing Stress and Anxiety

Effectively managing stress and anxiety is essential for promoting overall well-being and optimizing diabetes management. Consider incorporating the following stress management techniques into your daily routine:

- **Mindfulness and Meditation:** Practice mindfulness meditation, deep breathing exercises, and progressive muscle relaxation to promote relaxation, reduce stress, and enhance self-awareness.

- **Physical Activity:** Engage in regular physical activity, such as walking, yoga, tai chi, or dancing, to reduce stress hormones, release endorphins, and improve mood.

- **Healthy Coping Strategies:** Develop healthy coping strategies for managing stress, such as journaling, talking to a trusted friend or therapist, engaging in hobbies, and setting boundaries.

- **Time Management:** Prioritize tasks, set realistic goals, and delegate responsibilities to reduce feelings of overwhelm and maintain a sense of control.

- **Social Support:** Seek support from friends, family members, support groups, or mental health professionals to share experiences, seek guidance, and receive emotional support.

4.3 Importance of Mental Health Support

Recognizing the importance of mental health and seeking support when needed is critical for individuals living with type 2 diabetes. Diabetes management can be challenging and may contribute to feelings of stress, anxiety, depression, and burnout. It's essential to prioritize mental health and seek professional support if you experience persistent symptoms or difficulties coping with the demands of diabetes management.

Mental health professionals, including therapists, counselors, and psychologists, can provide valuable support, guidance, and coping strategies for managing stress, anxiety, and depression. They can help individuals develop resilience, cultivate healthy coping mechanisms, and improve overall quality of life.

In addition to professional support, peer support groups, online communities, and diabetes education programs can provide opportunities for connection, shared experiences, and emotional support. Connecting with others who understand the challenges of living with diabetes can help reduce feelings of isolation, increase motivation, and foster a sense of belonging.

Chapter 5: Sleep and Diabetes

Sleep plays a vital role in overall health and well-being, and its importance cannot be overstated, especially for individuals managing type 2 diabetes. In this expanded chapter, we will delve into the intricate relationship between sleep and diabetes, the impact of sleep quality on blood sugar control, strategies for improving sleep hygiene, and the significance of prioritizing adequate rest for optimal diabetes management.

5.1 Importance of Sleep for Diabetes Management

Quality sleep is essential for regulating various physiological processes, including metabolism, hormone regulation, immune function, and cognitive function. Sleep deprivation, poor sleep quality, and sleep disorders such as obstructive sleep apnea have been linked to insulin resistance, impaired glucose metabolism, weight gain, and increased risk of type 2 diabetes.

For individuals with type 2 diabetes, inadequate sleep can exacerbate insulin resistance, impair glycemic control, increase appetite and cravings for unhealthy foods, and elevate stress hormones such as cortisol, contributing to the vicious cycle of poor blood sugar management.

5.2 Tips for Improving Sleep Quality

Improving sleep quality and prioritizing adequate rest are essential components of diabetes management. Consider implementing the following tips to optimize your sleep hygiene:

- **Establish a Consistent Sleep Schedule:** Aim to go to bed and wake up at the same time each day, even on weekends, to regulate your body's internal clock and promote better sleep quality.

- **Create a Relaxing Bedtime Routine:** Develop a calming bedtime routine to signal to your body that it's time to wind down. Activities such as reading, taking a warm bath, practicing relaxation techniques, or gentle stretching can help prepare your mind and body for sleep.

- **Create a Comfortable Sleep Environment:** Ensure that your sleep environment is conducive to restful sleep. Keep your bedroom dark, quiet, and cool, invest in a comfortable mattress and pillows, and minimize distractions such as electronics and noise.

- **Limit Stimulants and Electronics Before Bed:** Avoid consuming caffeine, nicotine, and stimulating activities such as screen time (e.g., smartphones, computers, televisions) in the hours leading up to bedtime, as they can interfere with your ability to fall asleep and stay asleep.

- **Practice Healthy Lifestyle Habits:** Engage in regular physical activity, maintain a healthy diet, and manage stress through relaxation techniques and stress-reduction strategies to promote better sleep quality and overall well-being.

5.3 Establishing Healthy Sleep Habits

Establishing healthy sleep habits is essential for promoting restorative sleep and optimizing diabetes management. Consider the following strategies for improving your sleep habits:

- **Monitor Your Sleep Patterns:** Keep a sleep diary to track your sleep patterns, including bedtime, wake time, sleep duration, and perceived sleep quality. Identifying patterns and trends can help you pinpoint areas for improvement and make necessary adjustments to your sleep routine.

- **Seek Treatment for Sleep Disorders:** If you suspect you have a sleep disorder such as obstructive sleep apnea, restless legs syndrome, or insomnia, consult with a healthcare professional for evaluation and treatment options. Treating underlying sleep disorders can significantly improve sleep quality and overall health outcomes.

- **Practice Mindfulness and Relaxation Techniques:** Incorporate mindfulness meditation, deep breathing exercises, guided imagery, or progressive muscle relaxation into your bedtime routine to promote relaxation, reduce stress, and prepare your body for sleep.

Chapter 6: Meal Planning for Type 2 Diabetes

Meal planning is a cornerstone of effective type 2 diabetes management, providing individuals with the tools and knowledge to make healthy food choices, regulate blood sugar levels, and optimize overall health. In this comprehensive chapter, we will explore key principles of meal planning for type 2 diabetes, including carbohydrate management, portion control, glycemic index considerations, label reading, and creating personalized meal plans.

6.1 Understanding Carbohydrates, Proteins, and Fats

Carbohydrates, proteins, and fats are macronutrients that play crucial roles in energy metabolism and overall health. For individuals with type 2 diabetes, carbohydrate management is particularly important, as carbohydrates have the most significant impact on blood sugar levels. Understanding the sources and types of carbohydrates, including complex carbohydrates (e.g., whole grains, legumes, vegetables) and simple sugars (e.g., refined grains, sugary beverages), can help individuals make informed choices to control blood sugar levels.

Proteins and fats are essential for satiety, energy production, and nutrient absorption. Incorporating lean proteins (e.g., poultry, fish, tofu) and healthy fats (e.g., avocados, nuts, olive oil) into meals can help stabilize blood sugar levels, promote weight management, and support overall health.

6.2 Portion Control and Meal Timing

Portion control is critical for managing blood sugar levels and preventing overeating. Using visual cues, portion control tools, and measuring utensils can help individuals regulate portion sizes and prevent excessive calorie intake. Additionally, spacing meals evenly throughout the day and incorporating snacks as needed can help stabilize blood sugar levels and prevent fluctuations.

6.3 Glycemic Index and Glycemic Load

The glycemic index (GI) is a measure of how quickly carbohydrates in food raise blood sugar levels. Foods with a low GI (e.g., whole grains, non-starchy vegetables, legumes) are digested and absorbed more slowly, resulting in gradual increases in blood sugar levels. Incorporating low-GI foods into meals can help individuals maintain stable blood sugar levels and reduce the risk of hyperglycemia.

The glycemic load (GL) takes into account both the quantity and quality of carbohydrates in a serving of food. Foods with a low GL have a minimal impact on blood sugar levels, making them suitable choices for individuals with type 2 diabetes.

6.4 Reading Food Labels

Reading food labels is essential for individuals with type 2 diabetes to make informed choices about the nutritional content of foods. Paying attention to serving sizes, total carbohydrate content, fiber content, and added sugars can help individuals select foods that align with their dietary goals and blood sugar targets. Additionally, being mindful of portion sizes and serving sizes can prevent overconsumption and promote weight management.

6.5 Creating a Diabetes-Friendly Meal Plan

Creating a personalized diabetes-friendly meal plan involves incorporating a variety of nutrient-dense foods, balancing macronutrient intake, and considering individual preferences and dietary restrictions. A well-rounded meal plan should include:

- A variety of non-starchy vegetables, such as leafy greens, broccoli, peppers, and carrots, to provide essential vitamins, minerals, and antioxidants.

- Lean sources of protein, including poultry, fish, tofu, legumes, and low-fat dairy products, to support muscle health, satiety, and blood sugar control.

- Whole grains and complex carbohydrates, such as quinoa, brown rice, barley, and oats, to provide sustained energy and promote digestive health.

- Healthy fats from sources such as avocados, nuts, seeds, and olive oil, to support heart health, cognitive function, and nutrient absorption.

- Limited intake of added sugars, refined carbohydrates, processed foods, and high-fat foods, which can contribute to blood sugar spikes, weight gain, and cardiovascular risk.

Appendix Measurements Conversion

GAS MARK	DEGREE CELCIUS °C	DEGREE CELSIUS FAN °C	DEGREE FAHRENHEIT °F
1/4	110°C	100°C	225 °F
1/2	120°C	110°C	250 °F
1	140°C	120°C	275 °F
2	150°C	130°C	300 °F
3	170°C	140°C	325 °F
4	180°C	160°C	350 °F
5	190 °C	170°C	375 °F
6	200 °C	180°C	400 °F
7	220 °C	200°C	425 °F
8	230 °C	210°C	450 °F
9	240 °C	220°C	475 °F
10	260 °C	240°C	500 °F

Volume Conversions

Metric	Imperial	US Cups
250ml	8 fl oz	1 cup
180ml	6 fl oz	¾ cup
150 ml	5fl oz	⅔ cup
120ml	4 fl oz	½ cup
75ml	2 ½ fl oz	⅓ cup
60ml	2 fl oz	¼ cup
30 ml	1 fl oz	⅛ cup
15ml	½ fl oz	1 tablespoon

Grams	Pounds & Ounces
10 g	0.25 oz
20 g	0.75 oz
25 g	1 oz
40 g	1.50 oz
50 g	2 oz
60 g	2.5 oz
75 g	3 oz
110 g	4 oz
125 g	4.5 oz
150 g	5 oz
175 g	6 oz
200 g	7 oz
225 g	8 oz
250 g	9 oz
350 g	12 oz
450 g	1 lb
700 g	1 lb 8oz
900 g	2 lb
1.35 kg	3lb

Chapter 7: Recipes

Breakfast Recipes

1. Greek Yogurt Parfait

Preparation Time: 5 minutes
Cooking Time: None
Servings: 1

Ingredients:

- *1/2 cup Greek yogurt*
- *1/4 cup fresh berries (strawberries, blueberries, raspberries)*
- *2 tablespoons chopped nuts (almonds, walnuts)*
- *1 teaspoon honey or stevia (optional)*

Instructions:

1. In a clear glass, layer Greek yogurt, fresh berries, and chopped nuts.
2. Repeat the layering process until the glass is filled, ending with a layer of fresh berries and nuts on top.
3. If desired, drizzle honey or sprinkle stevia between the layers or on top for sweetness.

Nutritional Values (per serving):

- Calories: 200 kcal
- Carbohydrates: 15g
- Protein: 15g
- Fat: 10g

Glycemic Index: Low

2. Vegetable Omelette

Preparation Time: 10 minutes
Cooking Time: 10 minutes
Servings: 2

Ingredients:

- *4 eggs*
- *1/4 cup diced bell peppers*
- *1/4 cup diced onions*
- *1/4 cup chopped spinach*
- *Salt and pepper to taste*
- *Cooking spray or olive oil for cooking*

Instructions:

1. Whisk eggs in a bowl until well beaten. Season with salt and pepper.
2. Heat a non-stick skillet over medium heat and coat it with cooking spray or olive oil.
3. Add diced bell peppers and onions to the skillet. Sauté until they start to soften, about 2-3 minutes.
4. Add chopped spinach to the skillet and continue cooking until wilted, about 1-2 minutes.
5. Pour the beaten eggs into the skillet, ensuring they cover the vegetables evenly.
6. Allow the omelette to cook undisturbed for about 2-3 minutes until the edges begin to set.
7. Gently lift the edges of the omelette with a spatula and tilt the skillet to allow the uncooked eggs to flow to the bottom.
8. Once the omelette is mostly set but still slightly runny on top, fold it in half using the spatula.
9. Cook for another 1-2 minutes until the omelette is cooked through and the bottom is lightly golden.
10. Slide the omelette onto a plate and serve hot.

Nutritional Values (per serving):

- Calories: 200 kcal
- Carbohydrates: 5g
- Protein: 12g
- Fat: 14g

Glycemic Index: Low

3. Whole Grain Toast with Avocado

Preparation Time: 5 minutes
Cooking Time: None
Servings: 1

Ingredients:

- *1 slice whole grain bread, toasted*
- *1/2 ripe avocado, mashed*
- *Salt and pepper to taste*
- *Red pepper flakes (optional)*

Instructions:

1. Toast the slice of whole grain bread until it's golden brown and crispy.
2. While the toast is still warm, spread the mashed avocado evenly on top.
3. Season with salt, pepper, and red pepper flakes if desired, to add a little heat.
4. Serve immediately.

Nutritional Values (per serving):

- Calories: 200 kcal
- Carbohydrates: 15g
- Protein: 4g
- Fat: 15g

Glycemic Index: Low

4. Chia Seed Pudding

Preparation Time: 5 minutes (plus chilling time)
Cooking Time: None
Servings: 2

Ingredients:

- *1/4 cup chia seeds*

- *1 cup unsweetened almond milk*

- *1 tablespoon unsweetened cocoa powder (optional)*

- *1 tablespoon honey or stevia (optional)*

Instructions:

1. In a mixing bowl, combine chia seeds, almond milk, cocoa powder (if using), and sweetener (if desired).

2. Stir the mixture well until all ingredients are thoroughly combined.

3. Cover the bowl and refrigerate for at least 2 hours or overnight, allowing the chia seeds to absorb the liquid and thicken into pudding consistency.

4. Once chilled and set, stir the pudding again before serving.

5. Serve the chia seed pudding chilled, either as is or topped with fresh fruit, nuts, or a drizzle of honey for added flavor.

Nutritional Values (per serving):

- Calories: 150 kcal

- Carbohydrates: 10g

- Protein: 5g

- Fat: 10g

Glycemic Index: Low

5. Banana Nut Oatmeal

Preparation Time: 5 minutes
Cooking Time: 10 minutes
Servings: 2

Ingredients:

- *1 cup old-fashioned oats*
- *2 cups water or unsweetened almond milk*
- *1 ripe banana, mashed*
- *1/4 cup chopped nuts (walnuts, almonds)*
- *Cinnamon to taste*
- *Honey or stevia for sweetness (optional)*

Instructions:

1. In a saucepan, bring water or almond milk to a boil.
2. Stir in oats and reduce heat to low. Cook for about 5 minutes, stirring occasionally.
3. Add mashed banana and chopped nuts to the oatmeal and continue cooking until the desired consistency is reached, about 2-3 minutes.
4. Sprinkle with cinnamon and sweeten with honey or stevia if desired.
5. Remove from heat and let it sit for a minute to cool slightly before serving.
6. Serve warm in bowls.

Nutritional Values (per serving):

- Calories: 250 kcal
- Carbohydrates: 30g
- Protein: 7g
- Fat: 10g

Glycemic Index: Moderate (depending on banana ripeness)

6. Spinach and Feta Crustless Quiche

Preparation Time: 10 minutes
Cooking Time: 25 minutes
Servings: 4

Ingredients:

- *4 eggs*
- *1 cup fresh spinach, chopped*
- *1/4 cup crumbled feta cheese*
- *1/4 cup diced tomatoes*
- *Salt and pepper to taste*
- *Cooking spray or olive oil for greasing*

Instructions:

1. Preheat the oven to 350°F (175°C). Grease a pie dish with cooking spray or olive oil.
2. In a mixing bowl, whisk the eggs until well beaten. Season with salt and pepper.
3. Add the chopped spinach, crumbled feta cheese, and diced tomatoes to the eggs. Stir until well combined.
4. Pour the egg mixture into the prepared pie dish.
5. Bake in the preheated oven for about 25 minutes, or until the quiche is set and lightly golden on top.
6. Remove from the oven and let it cool for a few minutes before slicing.
7. Serve warm or at room temperature.

Nutritional Values (per serving):

- Calories: 150 kcal
- Carbohydrates: 3g
- Protein: 10g
- Fat: 10g

Glycemic Index: Low

7. Cottage Cheese and Fruit Bowl

Preparation Time: 5 minutes
Cooking Time: None
Servings: 1

Ingredients:

- *1/2 cup low-fat cottage cheese*
- *1/2 cup mixed fresh fruit (berries, melon, pineapple)*
- *1 tablespoon chopped nuts (almonds, walnuts)*
- *1 teaspoon honey or stevia (optional)*

Instructions:

1. In a serving bowl, spoon the low-fat cottage cheese.
2. Add the mixed fresh fruit on top of the cottage cheese.
3. Sprinkle chopped nuts over the fruit.
4. Drizzle honey or sprinkle stevia over the fruit and nuts for added sweetness, if desired.
5. Serve immediately and enjoy!

Nutritional Values (per serving):

- Calories: 200 kcal
- Carbohydrates: 15g
- Protein: 15g
- Fat: 10g

Glycemic Index: Low

8. Egg and Vegetable Breakfast Burrito

Preparation Time: 10 minutes
Cooking Time: 10 minutes
Servings: 2

Ingredients:

- *4 large eggs*
- *1/4 cup diced bell peppers*
- *1/4 cup diced onions*
- *1/4 cup diced tomatoes*
- *1/4 cup chopped spinach*
- *1/4 cup shredded cheese (cheddar, mozzarella)*
- *2 whole wheat or low-carb tortillas*
- *Salt and pepper to taste*
- *Cooking spray or olive oil for cooking*

Instructions:

1. In a bowl, whisk the eggs and season with salt and pepper.
2. Heat a non-stick skillet over medium heat and coat it with cooking spray or olive oil.
3. Add diced bell peppers and onions to the skillet. Sauté until they soften, about 2-3 minutes.
4. Add diced tomatoes and chopped spinach to the skillet. Cook until the spinach wilts, about 1-2 minutes.
5. Pour the whisked eggs into the skillet. Stir gently until the eggs are scrambled and cooked through.
6. Sprinkle shredded cheese over the scrambled eggs and vegetables. Allow the cheese to melt.
7. Warm the tortillas in a separate skillet or microwave.
8. Divide the egg and vegetable mixture evenly between the tortillas.
9. Roll up the tortillas, folding in the sides to enclose the filling. Serve warm.

Nutritional Values (per serving):

- Calories: 300 kcal
- Carbohydrates: 20g
- Protein: 15g
- Fat: 15g

Glycemic Index: Low

9. Peanut Butter Banana Smoothie

Preparation Time: 5 minutes
Cooking Time: None
Servings: 1

Ingredients:

- *1 ripe banana*
- *1 tablespoon natural peanut butter*
- *1/2 cup unsweetened almond milk*
- *1/2 cup plain Greek yogurt*
- *1 tablespoon flaxseeds or chia seeds*
- *Ice cubes (optional)*

Instructions:

1. Peel the ripe banana and break it into chunks.
2. In a blender, combine the banana chunks, natural peanut butter, unsweetened almond milk, plain Greek yogurt, and flaxseeds or chia seeds.
3. If you prefer a colder smoothie, add a handful of ice cubes to the blender.
4. Blend all the ingredients until smooth and creamy. If the smoothie is too thick, you can add more almond milk to reach your desired consistency.
5. Pour the smoothie into a glass and serve immediately.

Nutritional Values (per serving):

- Calories: 300 kcal
- Carbohydrates: 30g
- Protein: 15g
- Fat: 15g

Glycemic Index: Low

10. Turkey Sausage and Veggie Breakfast Casserole

Preparation Time: 15 minutes
Cooking Time: 35 minutes
Servings: 6

Ingredients:

- *6 eggs*
- *1/2 cup milk (or unsweetened almond milk)*
- *1 cup diced turkey sausage*
- *1/2 cup diced bell peppers*
- *1/2 cup diced onions*
- *1/2 cup diced tomatoes*
- *1 cup chopped spinach*
- *Salt and pepper to taste*
- *Cooking spray or olive oil for greasing*

Instructions:

1. Preheat the oven to 350°F (175°C). Grease a baking dish with cooking spray or olive oil.
2. In a mixing bowl, whisk together the eggs and milk until well combined. Season with salt and pepper.
3. Add the diced turkey sausage, bell peppers, onions, tomatoes, and chopped spinach to the egg mixture. Stir until evenly distributed.
4. Pour the mixture into the prepared baking dish, spreading it out evenly.
5. Bake in the preheated oven for about 35 minutes, or until the casserole is set and lightly golden on top.
6. Remove from the oven and let it cool for a few minutes before slicing.
7. Serve warm and enjoy!

Nutritional Values (per serving):

- Calories: 200 kcal
- Carbohydrates: 5g
- Protein: 15g
- Fat: 10g

Glycemic Index: Low

11. Smoked Salmon and Avocado Toast

Preparation Time: 10 minutes
Cooking Time: None
Servings: 2

Ingredients:

- *2 slices whole grain bread, toasted*
- *1 ripe avocado, sliced*
- *100g smoked salmon*
- *1 tablespoon capers (optional)*
- *Fresh dill, for garnish (optional)*
- *Lemon wedges, for serving (optional)*
- *Salt and pepper to taste*

Instructions:

1. Toast the slices of whole grain bread until golden brown and crispy.
2. While the toast is still warm, spread the sliced avocado evenly on top of each slice.
3. Place the smoked salmon slices on top of the avocado.
4. If using, sprinkle capers over the smoked salmon.
5. Season with salt and pepper to taste.
6. Garnish with fresh dill, if desired.
7. Serve immediately with lemon wedges on the side for extra flavor.

Nutritional Values (per serving):

- Calories: 250 kcal
- Carbohydrates: 15g
- Protein: 15g
- Fat: 15g

Glycemic Index: Low

12.Berry Protein Smoothie Bowl

Preparation Time: 10 minutes
Cooking Time: None
Servings: 1

Ingredients:

- *1 frozen banana, sliced*

- *1/2 cup mixed berries (strawberries, blueberries, raspberries)*

- *1/2 cup plain Greek yogurt*

- *1 scoop protein powder (vanilla or berry flavor)*

- *1/4 cup almond milk (or any milk of your choice)*

- *1 tablespoon honey or maple syrup (optional)*

- *Toppings: sliced fruits, granola, nuts, seeds, shredded coconut*

Instructions:

1. In a blender, combine the frozen banana slices, mixed berries, plain Greek yogurt, protein powder, almond milk, and honey or maple syrup if using.

2. Blend until smooth and creamy, adding more almond milk if necessary to achieve the desired consistency.

3. Pour the smoothie into a bowl.

4. Arrange the toppings of your choice over the smoothie bowl.

5. Serve immediately and enjoy!

Nutritional Values (per serving, excluding toppings):

- Calories: 300 kcal

- Carbohydrates: 40g

- Protein: 25g

- Fat: 5g

Glycemic Index: Moderate (depending on the fruits used)

13. Quinoa Breakfast Bowl with Almonds and Berries

Preparation Time: 15 minutes
Cooking Time: 15 minutes
Servings: 2

Ingredients:

- *1/2 cup quinoa, rinsed*
- *1 cup water*
- *1/2 cup almond milk (or any milk of your choice)*
- *1 tablespoon honey or maple syrup (optional)*
- *1/4 teaspoon ground cinnamon*
- *1/4 cup sliced almonds*
- *1/2 cup mixed berries (strawberries, blueberries, raspberries)*
- *Fresh mint leaves for garnish (optional)*

Instructions:

1. In a small saucepan, combine the quinoa and water. Bring to a boil, then reduce heat to low, cover, and simmer for about 12-15 minutes, or until the quinoa is cooked and the water is absorbed.
2. Once the quinoa is cooked, remove from heat and let it sit for a few minutes.
3. Fluff the quinoa with a fork and stir in the almond milk, honey or maple syrup (if using), and ground cinnamon.
4. Divide the quinoa into serving bowls.
5. Top each bowl of quinoa with sliced almonds and mixed berries.
6. Garnish with fresh mint leaves if desired.
7. Serve warm and enjoy!

Nutritional Values (per serving):

- Calories: 250 kcal
- Carbohydrates: 35g
- Protein: 8g
- Fat: 8g

Glycemic Index: Low

14.Egg Muffins with Spinach and Mushrooms

Preparation Time: 15 minutes
Cooking Time: 20 minutes
Servings: 6 muffins

Ingredients:

- *6 large eggs*
- *1 cup fresh spinach, chopped*
- *1/2 cup mushrooms, finely chopped*
- *1/4 cup shredded cheese (cheddar, mozzarella)*
- *1/4 cup milk (or unsweetened almond milk)*
- *Salt and pepper to taste*
- *Cooking spray or olive oil for greasing*

Instructions:

1. Preheat the oven to 350°F (175°C). Grease a muffin tin with cooking spray or olive oil.
2. In a mixing bowl, crack the eggs and whisk them together.
3. Add chopped spinach, mushrooms, shredded cheese, milk, salt, and pepper to the eggs. Stir until well combined.
4. Pour the egg mixture evenly into each muffin cup, filling them about 3/4 full.
5. Bake in the preheated oven for about 18-20 minutes, or until the egg muffins are set and lightly golden on top.
6. Remove from the oven and let them cool for a few minutes before removing them from the muffin tin.
7. Serve warm or at room temperature.

Nutritional Values (per muffin):

- Calories: 100 kcal
- Carbohydrates: 2g
- Protein: 8g
- Fat: 7g

Glycemic Index: Low

15. Low-Carb Breakfast Tacos

Preparation Time: 10 minutes
Cooking Time: 10 minutes
Servings: 2

Ingredients:

- *4 large eggs*
- *4 low-carb tortillas (look for options with almond flour or coconut flour)*
- *1/2 cup diced bell peppers*
- *1/2 cup diced onions*
- *1/2 cup diced tomatoes*
- *1/2 cup shredded cheese (cheddar, Monterey Jack)*
- *1 tablespoon olive oil*
- *Salt and pepper to taste*
- *Optional toppings: sliced avocado, salsa, sour cream, cilantro*

Instructions:

1. Heat olive oil in a skillet over medium heat.
2. Add diced bell peppers and onions to the skillet. Sauté until they start to soften, about 2-3 minutes.
3. Add diced tomatoes to the skillet and cook for another 1-2 minutes until slightly softened. Season with salt and pepper.
4. Push the vegetables to one side of the skillet and crack the eggs into the empty side.
5. Scramble the eggs until cooked through, then mix them with the sautéed vegetables.
6. Warm the low-carb tortillas in a separate skillet or microwave according to package instructions.
7. Divide the egg and vegetable mixture evenly between the tortillas.
8. Top each taco with shredded cheese and any optional toppings of your choice. Serve warm and enjoy!

Nutritional Values (per serving, 2 tacos):

- Calories: 300 kcal
- Carbohydrates: 15g
- Protein: 15g
- Fat: 20g

Glycemic Index: Low

Lunch Recipes

1. Grilled Chicken Salad with Balsamic Vinaigrette

Preparation Time: 15 minutes
Cooking Time: 15 minutes
Servings: 4

Ingredients:

- *2 boneless, skinless chicken breasts*
- *8 cups mixed salad greens*
- *1 cup cherry tomatoes, halved*
- *1/2 cucumber, sliced*
- *1/4 red onion, thinly sliced*
- *1/4 cup crumbled feta cheese*
- *1/4 cup balsamic vinegar*
- *2 tablespoons olive oil*
- *1 teaspoon Dijon mustard*
- *1 garlic clove, minced*
- *Salt and pepper to taste*

Instructions:

1. Preheat the grill to medium-high heat.
2. Season the chicken breasts with salt and pepper.
3. Grill the chicken breasts for about 6-8 minutes per side, or until they are cooked through and no longer pink in the center. Remove from the grill and let them rest for a few minutes before slicing.
4. In a small bowl, whisk together balsamic vinegar, olive oil, Dijon mustard, minced garlic, salt, and pepper to make the vinaigrette.
5. In a large salad bowl, combine the mixed greens, cherry tomatoes, sliced cucumber, and red onion.
6. Add the sliced grilled chicken on top of the salad.
7. Drizzle the balsamic vinaigrette over the salad and gently toss to coat.
8. Sprinkle crumbled feta cheese over the salad.
9. Serve immediately and enjoy!

Nutritional Values (per serving):

- Calories: 250 kcal

- Carbohydrates: 10g

- Protein: 25g

- Fat: 12g

Glycemic Index: Low

2. Quinoa and Vegetable Stir-Fry

Preparation Time: 15 minutes
Cooking Time: 20 minutes
Servings: 4

Ingredients:

- *1 cup quinoa, rinsed*

- *2 cups water or vegetable broth*

- *2 tablespoons olive oil*

- *2 cloves garlic, minced*

- *1 small onion, diced*

- *1 bell pepper, sliced*

- *1 cup broccoli florets*

- *1 cup sliced mushrooms*

- *1 medium carrot, julienned*

- *1 cup snow peas, trimmed*

- *2 tablespoons soy sauce (or tamari for gluten-free)*

- *1 tablespoon rice vinegar*

- *1 teaspoon sesame oil*

- *Salt and pepper to taste*

- *Optional toppings: sliced green onions, sesame seeds, chopped cilantro*

Instructions:

1. In a medium saucepan, combine quinoa and water or vegetable broth. Bring to a boil, then reduce heat to low, cover, and simmer for 15 minutes, or until the quinoa is cooked and liquid is absorbed. Remove from heat and let it sit for 5 minutes, then fluff with a fork.

2. In a large skillet or wok, heat olive oil over medium-high heat.

3. Add minced garlic and diced onion to the skillet. Stir-fry for 1-2 minutes until fragrant and translucent.

4. Add sliced bell pepper, broccoli florets, mushrooms, julienned carrot, and snow peas to the skillet. Stir-fry for 5-7 minutes until vegetables are tender-crisp.

5. In a small bowl, whisk together soy sauce, rice vinegar, and sesame oil.

6. Add cooked quinoa to the skillet with the vegetables. Pour the soy sauce mixture over the quinoa and vegetables.

7. Stir well to combine and heat through, about 2-3 minutes.

8. Season with salt and pepper to taste.

9. Remove from heat and garnish with sliced green onions, sesame seeds, and chopped cilantro if desired.

10. Serve hot and enjoy!

Nutritional Values (per serving):

3. Calories: 300 kcal

4. Carbohydrates: 40g

5. Protein: 10g

6. Fat: 12g

Glycemic Index: Low

3. Turkey and Avocado Wrap

Preparation Time: 10 minutes
Cooking Time: None
Servings: 2

Ingredients:

- *4 large whole wheat or low-carb tortillas*

- *8 slices turkey breast deli meat*

- *1 ripe avocado, sliced*

- *1/2 cup baby spinach leaves*

- *1/4 cup sliced red onion*

- *2 tablespoons hummus or mustard (optional)*

- *Salt and pepper to taste*

Instructions:

1. Lay out the tortillas on a clean work surface.

2. If using, spread hummus or mustard evenly over the tortillas.

3. Divide the turkey breast slices evenly among the tortillas, placing them in the center.

4. Layer sliced avocado, baby spinach leaves, and sliced red onion on top of the turkey slices.

5. Season with salt and pepper to taste.

6. Fold the sides of the tortillas inward, then roll up tightly from the bottom to create wraps.

7. Slice each wrap in half diagonally, if desired.

8. Serve immediately, or wrap tightly in foil or parchment paper for on-the-go lunches.

Nutritional Values (per serving, 1 wrap):

- Calories: 300 kcal

- Carbohydrates: 25g

- Protein: 20g

- Fat: 15g

Glycemic Index: Low

4. Salmon and Asparagus Foil Packets

Preparation Time: 10 minutes
Cooking Time: 20 minutes
Servings: 2

Ingredients:

- *2 salmon fillets, skinless*

- *1 bunch asparagus, trimmed*

- *2 tablespoons olive oil*

- *2 cloves garlic, minced*

- *1 lemon, thinly sliced*

- *Salt and pepper to taste*

- *Fresh herbs (such as dill, parsley) for garnish (optional)*

Instructions:

1. Preheat the oven to 400°F (200°C).

2. Cut two large pieces of aluminum foil, enough to wrap around each salmon fillet and asparagus bunch.

3. Place each salmon fillet in the center of a piece of foil.

4. Arrange trimmed asparagus spears around the salmon fillets.

5. Drizzle olive oil over the salmon and asparagus.

6. Sprinkle minced garlic over the salmon and asparagus.

7. Season everything with salt and pepper to taste.

8. Place lemon slices on top of the salmon fillets.

9. Fold the foil over the salmon and asparagus to create sealed packets.

10. Place the foil packets on a baking sheet and bake in the preheated oven for 15-20 minutes, or until the salmon is cooked through and the asparagus is tender.

11. Carefully open the foil packets and transfer the salmon and asparagus to serving plates.

12. Garnish with fresh herbs if desired. Serve hot and enjoy!

Nutritional Values (per serving):

- Calories: 300 kcal

- Carbohydrates: 8g

- Protein: y 30g

- Fat: 18g

Glycemic Index: Low

5. Cauliflower Rice Burrito Bowl

Preparation Time: 15 minutes
Cooking Time: 20 minutes
Servings: 4

Ingredients:

- *1 head cauliflower*

- *1 tablespoon olive oil*

- *1 onion, diced*

- *2 cloves garlic, minced*

- *1 bell pepper, diced*

- *1 cup corn kernels (fresh, frozen, or canned)*

- *1 cup black beans, drained and rinsed*

- *1 teaspoon chili powder*

- *1 teaspoon ground cumin*

- *Salt and pepper to taste*

- *Juice of 1 lime*

- *1/4 cup chopped fresh cilantro*

- *Optional toppings: avocado slices, diced tomatoes, shredded cheese, Greek yogurt or sour cream, salsa*

Instructions:

1. Cut the cauliflower into florets and pulse in a food processor until it resembles rice-like grains.

2. Heat olive oil in a large skillet over medium heat.

3. Add diced onion and minced garlic to the skillet. Sauté until fragrant and translucent, about 2-3 minutes.

4. Add diced bell pepper to the skillet and cook for another 3-4 minutes until softened.

5. Stir in the cauliflower rice, corn kernels, and black beans.

6. Season with chili powder, ground cumin, salt, and pepper. Stir well to combine.

7. Cook for 5-7 minutes, stirring occasionally, until the cauliflower rice is tender and heated through.

8. Remove from heat and stir in the lime juice and chopped cilantro.

9. Taste and adjust seasoning if necessary.

10. Divide the cauliflower rice mixture into serving bowls.

11. Top each bowl with avocado slices, diced tomatoes, shredded cheese, Greek yogurt or sour cream, and salsa as desired.

12. Serve hot and enjoy!

Nutritional Values (per serving):

- Calories: 200 kcal

- Carbohydrates: 30g

- Protein: 10g

- Fat: 5g

Glycemic Index: Low

6. Lentil Soup with Spinach and Tomatoes

Preparation Time: 15 minutes
Cooking Time: 45 minutes
Servings: 6

Ingredients:

- *1 cup dried lentils, rinsed and drained*

- *1 tablespoon olive oil*

- *1 onion, chopped*

- *2 cloves garlic, minced*

- *2 carrots, diced*

- *2 celery stalks, diced*
- *1 can (14 oz) diced tomatoes, undrained*
- *6 cups vegetable broth or water*
- *2 cups fresh spinach leaves, chopped*
- *1 teaspoon dried thyme*
- *1 teaspoon dried oregano*
- *Salt and pepper to taste*
- *Optional garnish: fresh parsley, grated Parmesan cheese*

Instructions:

1. In a large soup pot, heat olive oil over medium heat.
2. Add chopped onion and minced garlic to the pot. Sauté until onion is translucent and garlic is fragrant, about 2-3 minutes.
3. Add diced carrots and celery to the pot. Cook for another 3-4 minutes until vegetables begin to soften.
4. Stir in dried lentils, diced tomatoes (with their juices), vegetable broth or water, dried thyme, and dried oregano.
5. Bring the soup to a boil, then reduce heat to low. Cover and simmer for 30-40 minutes, or until lentils are tender.
6. Once lentils are cooked, stir in chopped spinach leaves. Cook for an additional 5 minutes until spinach wilts.
7. Season the soup with salt and pepper to taste.
8. Serve hot, garnished with fresh parsley and grated Parmesan cheese if desired.
9. Enjoy your delicious Lentil Soup with Spinach and Tomatoes!

Nutritional Values (per serving):

- Calories: 200 kcal
- Carbohydrates: 30g
- Protein: 12g
- Fat: 3g

Glycemic Index: Low

7. Zucchini Noodles with Pesto and Cherry Tomatoes

Preparation Time: 15 minutes
Cooking Time: 10 minutes
Servings: 4

Ingredients:

- *4 medium zucchini*
- *1 cup cherry tomatoes, halved*
- *1/4 cup prepared pesto sauce*
- *2 tablespoons olive oil*
- *2 cloves garlic, minced*
- *Salt and pepper to taste*
- *Grated Parmesan cheese for garnish (optional)*
- *Fresh basil leaves for garnish (optional)*

Instructions:

1. Trim the ends of the zucchini and spiralize them into noodles using a spiralizer. Alternatively, you can use a vegetable peeler to create zucchini ribbons.

2. Heat olive oil in a large skillet over medium heat.

3. Add minced garlic to the skillet and sauté for about 1 minute until fragrant.

4. Add cherry tomatoes to the skillet and cook for 2-3 minutes until they start to soften.

5. Add zucchini noodles to the skillet and toss with the tomatoes and garlic.

6. Cook the zucchini noodles for 2-3 minutes until they are just tender but still slightly crisp.

7. Stir in the prepared pesto sauce and toss until the zucchini noodles are evenly coated.

8. Season with salt and pepper to taste.

9. Remove from heat and transfer the zucchini noodles to serving plates.

10. Garnish with grated Parmesan cheese and fresh basil leaves if desired.

11. Serve immediately and enjoy!

Nutritional Values (per serving):

- Calories: 150 kcal
- Carbohydrates: 8g
- Protein: 3g
- Fat: 12g

Glycemic Index: Low

8. Tofu and Vegetable Stir-Fry with Brown Rice

Preparation Time: 15 minutes
Cooking Time: 20 minutes
Servings: 4

Ingredients:

- *1 cup brown rice*
- *2 cups water*
- *14 oz (400g) firm tofu, pressed and cubed*
- *2 tablespoons soy sauce*
- *1 tablespoon sesame oil*
- *1 tablespoon cornstarch*
- *2 tablespoons vegetable oil*
- *2 cloves garlic, minced*
- *1 onion, thinly sliced*
- *2 carrots, julienned*
- *1 bell pepper, thinly sliced*
- *1 cup broccoli florets*
- *1 cup snap peas*
- *Salt and pepper to taste*
- *Optional garnish: sesame seeds, chopped green onions*

Instructions:

1. Rinse the brown rice under cold water until the water runs clear. In a medium saucepan, combine the brown rice and water. Bring to a boil, then reduce the heat to low, cover, and simmer for 40-45 minutes, or until the rice is tender and the water is absorbed. Remove from heat and let it sit covered for 5 minutes, then fluff with a fork.

2. In a small bowl, whisk together soy sauce, sesame oil, and cornstarch until well combined. Add the cubed tofu to the bowl and toss gently to coat. Set aside to marinate for about 10 minutes.

3. Heat vegetable oil in a large skillet or wok over medium-high heat. Add minced garlic and sliced onion to the skillet. Stir-fry for 1-2 minutes until fragrant and translucent.

4. Add julienned carrots, sliced bell pepper, broccoli florets, and snap peas to the skillet. Stir-fry for 3-4 minutes until the vegetables are tender-crisp.

5. Push the vegetables to one side of the skillet and add the marinated tofu to the other side. Cook the tofu for 3-4 minutes until golden brown on all sides.

6. Stir everything together in the skillet until well combined. Season with salt and pepper to taste.

7. Remove from heat and serve the tofu and vegetable stir-fry over cooked brown rice.

8. Garnish with sesame seeds and chopped green onions if desired.

9. Serve hot and enjoy!

Nutritional Values (per serving):

- Calories: 350 kcal

- Carbohydrates: 45g

- Protein: 15g

- Fat: 12g

Glycemic Index: Low

9. Chickpea Salad with Cucumber and Feta

Preparation Time: 15 minutes
Cooking Time: 0 minutes
Servings: 4

Ingredients:

- *2 cans (15 oz each) chickpeas, drained and rinsed*

- *1 cucumber, diced*

- *1/2 red onion, finely chopped*

- *1/2 cup crumbled feta cheese*

- *1/4 cup fresh parsley, chopped*

- *2 tablespoons olive oil*

- *2 tablespoons lemon juice*

- *1 teaspoon dried oregano*

- *Salt and pepper to taste*

Instructions:

1. In a large mixing bowl, combine the drained and rinsed chickpeas, diced cucumber, finely chopped red onion, crumbled feta cheese, and chopped fresh parsley.

2. In a small bowl, whisk together the olive oil, lemon juice, dried oregano, salt, and pepper to make the dressing.

3. Pour the dressing over the chickpea salad mixture.

4. Toss gently until all the ingredients are evenly coated with the dressing.

5. Taste and adjust seasoning if necessary.

6. Refrigerate the chickpea salad for at least 30 minutes before serving to allow the flavors to meld together.

7. Serve chilled and enjoy!

Nutritional Values (per serving):

- Calories: 250 kcal

- Carbohydrates: 30g

- Protein: 10g

- Fat: 10g

Glycemic Index: Low

10. Eggplant Parmesan with Whole Wheat

Preparation Time: 30 minutes
Cooking Time: 45 minutes
Servings: 4

Ingredients:

- *1 large eggplant, sliced into 1/2-inch rounds*

- *1 cup whole wheat breadcrumbs*

- *2 eggs, beaten*

- *1 cup marinara sauce*

- *1 cup shredded mozzarella cheese*

- *1/4 cup grated Parmesan cheese*

- *2 tablespoons olive oil*

- *1 teaspoon dried oregano*

- *1 teaspoon dried basil*

- *Salt and pepper to taste*

- *Fresh basil leaves for garnish (optional)*

Instructions:

1. Preheat the oven to 400°F (200°C). Grease a baking sheet with olive oil or line it with parchment paper.

2. In a shallow dish, combine whole wheat breadcrumbs with dried oregano, dried basil, salt, and pepper.

3. Dip each eggplant slice into the beaten eggs, then coat with the seasoned breadcrumbs, pressing gently to adhere.

4. Place the breaded eggplant slices on the prepared baking sheet in a single layer.

5. Bake in the preheated oven for 20-25 minutes, flipping halfway through, until the eggplant is golden brown and tender.

6. Remove the baking sheet from the oven and reduce the oven temperature to 350°F (175°C).

7. Spread a thin layer of marinara sauce on the bottom of a baking dish.

8. Arrange half of the baked eggplant slices in the baking dish, overlapping slightly.

9. Spoon more marinara sauce over the eggplant slices, then sprinkle with shredded mozzarella cheese and grated Parmesan cheese.

10. Repeat with the remaining eggplant slices, marinara sauce, and cheeses.

11. Bake in the preheated oven for 20-25 minutes, until the cheese is melted and bubbly.

12. Remove from the oven and let it cool for a few minutes before serving.

13. Garnish with fresh basil leaves if desired.

14. Serve hot and enjoy!

Nutritional Values (per serving):

- Calories: 300 kcal

- Carbohydrates: 25g

- Protein: 15g

- Fat: 15g

Glycemic Index: Medium

11. Shrimp and Vegetable Skewers with Quinoa

Preparation Time: 20 minutes
Cooking Time: 15 minutes
Servings: 4

Ingredients:

- *1 pound large shrimp, peeled and deveined*

- *2 bell peppers (any color), cut into chunks*

- *1 red onion, cut into chunks*

- *1 zucchini, sliced into rounds*

- *1 yellow squash, sliced into rounds*

- *1 cup quinoa, rinsed*

- *2 cups water or vegetable broth*

- *2 tablespoons olive oil*

- *2 cloves garlic, minced*

- *1 teaspoon dried thyme*

- *Salt and pepper to taste*

- *Wooden or metal skewers*

Instructions:

1. If using wooden skewers, soak them in water for at least 30 minutes to prevent burning.

2. In a medium saucepan, combine quinoa and water or vegetable broth. Bring to a boil, then reduce heat to low, cover, and simmer for 15 minutes, or until the quinoa is cooked and liquid is absorbed. Remove from heat and let it sit for 5 minutes, then fluff with a fork.

3. In a small bowl, whisk together olive oil, minced garlic, dried thyme, salt, and pepper to make the marinade.

4. Thread shrimp, bell peppers, red onion, zucchini, and yellow squash onto skewers, alternating the ingredients.

5. Brush the marinade over the shrimp and vegetables on the skewers, coating them evenly.

6. Preheat the grill or grill pan to medium-high heat.

7. Place the skewers on the grill and cook for 2-3 minutes per side, or until the shrimp is pink and opaque and the vegetables are tender and slightly charred.

8. Remove the skewers from the grill and let them rest for a few minutes.

9. Serve the shrimp and vegetable skewers over cooked quinoa.

10. Garnish with fresh herbs or a squeeze of lemon juice if desired.

11. Serve hot and enjoy!

Nutritional Values (per serving):

- Calories: 350 kcal

- Carbohydrates: 35g

- Protein:25g

- Fat: 2g

Glycemic Index: Low

12. Greek Salad with Grilled Chicken

Preparation Time: 20 minutes
Cooking Time: 15 minutes
Servings: 4

Ingredients:

- *2 boneless, skinless chicken breasts*
- *1 head romaine lettuce, chopped*
- *1 cucumber, diced*
- *1 bell pepper (any color), diced*
- *1 cup cherry tomatoes, halved*
- *1/2 red onion, thinly sliced*
- *1/2 cup Kalamata olives, pitted*
- *1/2 cup crumbled feta cheese*
- *2 tablespoons olive oil*
- *2 tablespoons red wine vinegar*
- *1 teaspoon dried oregano*
- *Salt and pepper to taste*
- *Optional garnish: fresh oregano leaves, lemon wedges*

Instructions:

1. Preheat the grill to medium-high heat.

2. Season the chicken breasts with salt, pepper, and dried oregano.

3. Grill the chicken breasts for about 6-8 minutes per side, or until they are cooked through and no longer pink in the center. Remove from the grill and let them rest for a few minutes before slicing.

4. In a large salad bowl, combine the chopped romaine lettuce, diced cucumber, diced bell pepper, halved cherry tomatoes, thinly sliced red onion, and pitted Kalamata olives.

5. In a small bowl, whisk together olive oil, red wine vinegar, dried oregano, salt, and pepper to make the dressing.

6. Pour the dressing over the salad ingredients in the bowl and toss gently to coat.

7. Divide the salad among serving plates.

8. Slice the grilled chicken breasts and arrange them on top of the salads.

9. Sprinkle crumbled feta cheese over the salads.

10. Garnish with fresh oregano leaves and serve with lemon wedges if desired. Serve immediately and enjoy!

Nutritional Values (per serving):

- Calories: 300 kcal
- Carbohydrates: 12g
- Protein: 25g
- Fat: 18g

Glycemic Index: Low

13. Black Bean and Corn Quesadillas

Preparation Time: 15 minutes
Cooking Time: 10 minutes
Servings: 4

Ingredients:

- *8 medium flour tortillas*
- *1 can (15 oz) black beans, drained and rinsed*
- *1 cup frozen corn kernels, thawed*
- *1 bell pepper, diced*
- *1 small onion, diced*
- *2 cloves garlic, minced*
- *1 teaspoon ground cumin*
- *1 teaspoon chili powder*
- *1 cup shredded Monterey Jack or cheddar cheese*
- *2 tablespoons olive oil*
- *Salt and pepper to taste*
- *Salsa, guacamole, sour cream, for serving (optional)*

Instructions:

1. In a large skillet, heat 1 tablespoon of olive oil over medium heat.
2. Add diced onion and minced garlic to the skillet. Sauté until onion is translucent and garlic is fragrant, about 2-3 minutes.
3. Add diced bell pepper to the skillet and cook for another 3-4 minutes until softened.
4. Stir in black beans, thawed corn kernels, ground cumin, and chili powder. Cook for 2-3 minutes until heated through. Season with salt and pepper to taste. Remove from heat and set aside.
5. Heat a clean skillet or griddle over medium heat.

6. Brush one side of each tortilla lightly with olive oil.

7. Place one tortilla, oiled side down, on the skillet or griddle.

8. Spoon a layer of the black bean and corn mixture evenly over the tortilla.

9. Sprinkle shredded cheese over the black bean and corn mixture.

10. Top with another tortilla, oiled side up.

11. Cook for 2-3 minutes until the bottom tortilla is golden brown and crispy, and the cheese is melted.

12. Carefully flip the quesadilla and cook for another 2-3 minutes on the other side.

13. Remove from the skillet and let it cool for a minute before slicing into wedges.

14. Repeat with the remaining tortillas and filling ingredients.

15. Serve the black bean and corn quesadillas warm with salsa, guacamole, sour cream, or your favorite toppings.

16. Enjoy!

Nutritional Values (per serving):

- Calories: 350 kcal

- Carbohydrates: 40g

- Protein: 15g

- Fat: 15g

Glycemic Index: Low

14. Spinach and Mushroom Frittata

Preparation Time: 15 minutes
Cooking Time: 20 minutes
Servings: 4

Ingredients:

- *8 large eggs*

- *1 cup fresh spinach leaves, chopped*

- *1 cup mushrooms, sliced*

- *1/2 onion, diced*

- *2 cloves garlic, minced*

- *1/2 cup shredded cheese (such as cheddar or mozzarella)*

- *2 tablespoons olive oil*

- *Salt and pepper to taste*

- *Fresh herbs for garnish (optional)*

Instructions:

1. Preheat the oven to 375°F (190°C).

2. In a large bowl, whisk together the eggs until well beaten. Season with salt and pepper to taste.

3. Heat olive oil in a large oven-safe skillet over medium heat.

4. Add diced onion and minced garlic to the skillet. Sauté until the onion is translucent and the garlic is fragrant, about 2-3 minutes.

5. Add sliced mushrooms to the skillet and cook for another 3-4 minutes until they start to brown.

6. Stir in chopped spinach leaves and cook for 1-2 minutes until wilted.

7. Spread the vegetables evenly in the skillet.

8. Pour the beaten eggs over the vegetables in the skillet, making sure they are evenly distributed.

9. Cook the frittata on the stovetop for 3-4 minutes, until the edges start to set.

10. Sprinkle shredded cheese evenly over the top of the frittata.

11. Transfer the skillet to the preheated oven and bake for 12-15 minutes, or until the frittata is set in the center and the top is golden brown.

12. Remove from the oven and let it cool for a few minutes.

13. Slice the frittata into wedges.

14. Garnish with fresh herbs if desired.

15. Serve warm or at room temperature.

16. Enjoy!

Nutritional Values (per serving):

- Calories: 200 kcal

- Carbohydrates: 4g

- Protein: 12g

- Fat: 15g

Glycemic Index: Low

15.Asian-Inspired Tuna Salad with Sesame Dressing

Preparation Time: 15 minutes
Cooking Time: 0 minutes
Servings: 4

Ingredients:

- *2 cans (5 oz each) tuna in water, drained*
- *4 cups mixed salad greens (such as lettuce, spinach, or arugula)*
- *1 cucumber, thinly sliced*
- *1 carrot, grated*
- *1/4 cup sliced almonds, toasted*
- *2 green onions, thinly sliced*
- *2 tablespoons sesame seeds, toasted*

For the Sesame Dressing:

- *3 tablespoons soy sauce*
- *2 tablespoons rice vinegar*
- *1 tablespoon sesame oil*
- *1 tablespoon honey or maple syrup*
- *1 teaspoon grated fresh ginger*
- *1 clove garlic, minced*
- *Salt and pepper to taste*

Instructions:

1. In a large mixing bowl, combine the drained tuna, mixed salad greens, sliced cucumber, grated carrot, sliced almonds, and thinly sliced green onions.
2. In a small bowl, whisk together the soy sauce, rice vinegar, sesame oil, honey or maple syrup, grated fresh ginger, minced garlic, salt, and pepper to make the sesame dressing.
3. Pour the sesame dressing over the tuna salad mixture in the large bowl.
4. Toss gently to coat all the ingredients evenly with the dressing.
5. Divide the Asian-Inspired Tuna Salad among serving plates or bowls.
6. Sprinkle toasted sesame seeds over each serving.
7. Serve immediately and enjoy!

Nutritional Values (per serving):

- Calories: 200 kcal

- Carbohydrates: 10g

- Protein: 20g

- Fat: 10g

Glycemic Index: Low

Dinner

1. Grilled Salmon with Asparagus

Preparation Time: 10 minutes
Cooking Time: 10 minutes
Servings: 4

Ingredients:

- *4 salmon fillets (about 6 oz each)*
- *1 lb fresh asparagus, trimmed*
- *2 tablespoons olive oil*
- *2 cloves garlic, minced*
- *1 lemon, thinly sliced*
- *Salt and pepper to taste*
- *Fresh herbs (such as dill or parsley) for garnish (optional)*

Instructions:

1. Preheat your grill to medium-high heat.
2. In a small bowl, mix together the olive oil, minced garlic, salt, and pepper to create a marinade.
3. Place the salmon fillets and trimmed asparagus spears in a shallow dish. Pour the marinade over them, ensuring they are evenly coated. Let them marinate for about 10 minutes.
4. While the grill is heating up, arrange lemon slices on top of each salmon fillet.
5. Once the grill is hot, place the salmon fillets and asparagus spears directly on the grill.
6. Grill the salmon for about 4-5 minutes per side, or until it flakes easily with a fork and is cooked to your desired level of doneness.
7. Grill the asparagus for about 5-7 minutes, turning occasionally, until they are tender and slightly charred.
8. Once the salmon and asparagus are cooked, remove them from the grill.
9. Serve the grilled salmon and asparagus hot, garnished with fresh herbs if desired.
10. Enjoy your delicious and nutritious meal!

Nutritional Values (per serving):

- Calories: 300 kcal
- Carbohydrates: 6g
- Protein: 30g

- Fat: 18g

Glycemic Index: Low

2. Turkey Meatballs with Zucchini Noodles

Preparation Time: 20 minutes
Cooking Time: 20 minutes
Servings: 4

Ingredients:

For Turkey Meatballs:

- *1 lb ground turkey*
- *1/2 cup breadcrumbs (whole wheat for a lower glycemic option)*
- *1/4 cup grated Parmesan cheese*
- *1 large egg*
- *2 cloves garlic, minced*
- *1 teaspoon dried oregano*
- *Salt and pepper to taste*
- *2 tablespoons olive oil*

For Zucchini Noodles:

- *4 medium-sized zucchinis, spiralized*
- *1 tablespoon olive oil*
- *Salt and pepper to taste*

For Tomato Sauce:

- *1 can (14 oz) crushed tomatoes*
- *2 cloves garlic, minced*
- *1 teaspoon dried basil*
- *1 teaspoon dried oregano*
- *Salt and pepper to taste*

Instructions:

1. Preheat the oven to 375°F (190°C).

2. In a large mixing bowl, combine ground turkey, breadcrumbs, grated Parmesan cheese, egg, minced garlic, dried oregano, salt, and pepper. Mix until well combined.

3. Form the mixture into meatballs, about 1 inch in diameter.

4. Heat olive oil in an oven-safe skillet over medium-high heat. Brown the meatballs on all sides, about 2-3 minutes per side.

5. Transfer the skillet to the preheated oven and bake the meatballs for 12-15 minutes or until they are cooked through.

6. While the meatballs are baking, prepare the zucchini noodles. In a separate skillet, heat olive oil over medium heat. Add spiralized zucchini and sauté for 3-5 minutes until just tender. Season with salt and pepper.

7. In another saucepan, combine crushed tomatoes, minced garlic, dried basil, dried oregano, salt, and pepper. Simmer for 10-15 minutes, stirring occasionally.

8. Once the meatballs are done, remove them from the oven.

9. Serve the turkey meatballs on a bed of zucchini noodles, topped with tomato sauce.

10. Garnish with additional Parmesan cheese and fresh basil if desired.

11. Enjoy your healthy and delicious turkey meatballs with zucchini noodles!

Nutritional Values (per serving):

- Calories: 350 kcal
- Carbohydrates: 15g
- Protein: 25g
- Fat: 20g

Glycemic Index: Low (especially with whole wheat breadcrumbs)

3. Baked Chicken Breast with Roasted Vegetables

Preparation Time: 15 minutes
Cooking Time: 25 minutes
Servings: 4

Ingredients:

- *4 boneless, skinless chicken breasts*
- *2 medium potatoes, diced*
- *2 carrots, sliced*
- *1 red bell pepper, chopped*
- *1 yellow bell pepper, chopped*
- *1 zucchini, sliced*
- *1 onion, sliced*

- *4 cloves garlic, minced*
- *2 tablespoons olive oil*
- *1 teaspoon dried thyme*
- *1 teaspoon dried rosemary*
- *Salt and pepper to taste*
- *Fresh parsley for garnish (optional)*

Instructions:

1. Preheat the oven to 400°F (200°C).
2. Season the chicken breasts with salt, pepper, dried thyme, and dried rosemary on both sides.
3. Place the seasoned chicken breasts in a baking dish lightly coated with olive oil or lined with parchment paper.
4. In a large mixing bowl, combine diced potatoes, sliced carrots, chopped red bell pepper, chopped yellow bell pepper, sliced zucchini, sliced onion, minced garlic, olive oil, salt, and pepper. Toss to coat the vegetables evenly with the oil and seasonings.
5. Spread the seasoned vegetables around the chicken breasts in the baking dish.
6. Bake in the preheated oven for about 20-25 minutes, or until the chicken is cooked through and the vegetables are tender, stirring the vegetables halfway through.
7. Remove from the oven and let it rest for a few minutes before serving.
8. Garnish with fresh parsley if desired.
9. Serve the baked chicken breasts with roasted vegetables hot.
10. Enjoy your nutritious and delicious meal!

Nutritional Values (per serving):

- Calories: 300 kcal
- Carbohydrates: 20g
- Protein: 30g
- Fat: 10g

Glycemic Index: Medium

4. Quinoa-Stuffed Bell Peppers

Preparation Time: 20 minutes
Cooking Time: 40 minutes
Servings: 4

Ingredients:

- *4 large bell peppers (any color), tops removed and seeds discarded*
- *1 cup quinoa, rinsed*
- *2 cups vegetable broth or water*
- *1 tablespoon olive oil*
- *1 small onion, finely chopped*
- *2 cloves garlic, minced*
- *1 carrot, finely chopped*
- *1 zucchini, finely chopped*
- *1 cup canned black beans, drained and rinsed*
- *1 cup diced tomatoes (canned or fresh)*
- *1 teaspoon ground cumin*
- *1 teaspoon chili powder*
- *Salt and pepper to taste*
- *1/2 cup shredded cheese (such as cheddar or mozzarella), optional*
- *Fresh cilantro or parsley for garnish, optional*

Instructions:

1. Preheat the oven to 375°F (190°C).

2. In a medium saucepan, bring the vegetable broth or water to a boil. Add quinoa, reduce heat to low, cover, and simmer for about 15-20 minutes, or until the quinoa is cooked and liquid is absorbed. Remove from heat and set aside.

3. In a large skillet, heat olive oil over medium heat. Add chopped onion and garlic, and cook until softened, about 2-3 minutes.

4. Add chopped carrot and zucchini to the skillet, and cook for another 5 minutes until vegetables are tender.

5. Stir in black beans, diced tomatoes, ground cumin, chili powder, salt, and pepper. Cook for 2-3 minutes until heated through.

6. Remove the skillet from heat and stir in cooked quinoa until well combined.

7. Stuff each bell pepper with the quinoa and vegetable mixture, pressing down gently to pack it in.

8. Place the stuffed bell peppers in a baking dish. If desired, sprinkle shredded cheese over the top of each stuffed pepper.

9. Cover the baking dish with aluminum foil and bake in the preheated oven for about 25-30 minutes, or until the bell peppers are tender.

10. Remove the foil and bake for an additional 5-10 minutes to melt the cheese and allow the tops to brown slightly.

11. Remove from the oven and let it cool for a few minutes before serving.

12. Garnish with fresh cilantro or parsley if desired.

13. Serve the quinoa-stuffed bell peppers hot.

14. Enjoy your nutritious and delicious meal!

Nutritional Values (per serving, without cheese):

- Calories: 300 kcal

- Carbohydrates: 50g

- Protein: 12g

- Fat: 6g

Glycemic Index: Low

5. Stir-Fried Tofu with Broccoli and Brown Rice

Preparation Time: 15 minutes
Cooking Time: 15 minutes
Servings: 4

Ingredients:

- *1 block (14 oz) firm tofu, drained and pressed*

- *2 cups broccoli florets*

- *2 cups cooked brown rice*

- *3 tablespoons soy sauce (reduced-sodium if preferred)*

- *2 tablespoons hoisin sauce*

- *2 cloves garlic, minced*

- *1 tablespoon ginger, minced*

- *2 tablespoons sesame oil*

- *1 tablespoon olive oil*

- *1 teaspoon cornstarch mixed with 2 tablespoons water*

- *Salt and pepper to taste*

- *Sesame seeds for garnish (optional)*

- *Sliced green onions for garnish (optional)*

Instructions:

1. Prepare the tofu by cutting it into cubes or rectangles. Press the tofu between paper towels or kitchen towels to remove excess moisture.

2. In a small bowl, mix soy sauce, hoisin sauce, minced garlic, minced ginger, and cornstarch slurry. Set aside.

3. Heat olive oil in a large skillet or wok over medium-high heat.

4. Add the tofu cubes to the skillet and cook until they are golden brown and crispy on all sides, about 5-7 minutes. Remove tofu from the skillet and set aside.

5. In the same skillet, add sesame oil and broccoli florets. Stir-fry for about 3-4 minutes until the broccoli is bright green and slightly tender.

6. Return the tofu to the skillet with the broccoli.

7. Pour the sauce mixture over the tofu and broccoli. Stir well to coat evenly.

8. Cook for an additional 2-3 minutes until the sauce thickens and coats the tofu and broccoli.

9. Season with salt and pepper to taste.

10. Serve the stir-fried tofu and broccoli over cooked brown rice.

11. Garnish with sesame seeds and sliced green onions if desired.

12. Enjoy your delicious and nutritious stir-fried tofu with broccoli and brown rice!

Nutritional Values (per serving):

- Calories: 300 kcal

- Carbohydrates: 30g

- Protein: 15g

- Fat: 15g

Glycemic Index: Low

6. Lemon Herb Roasted Chicken Thighs with Cauliflower Mash

Preparation Time: 15 minutes
Cooking Time: 40 minutes
Servings: 4

Ingredients:

- *4 chicken thighs, bone-in and skin-on*
- *2 lemons, juiced and zested*
- *4 cloves garlic, minced*
- *2 tablespoons olive oil*
- *1 tablespoon fresh rosemary, chopped*
- *1 tablespoon fresh thyme leaves*
- *Salt and pepper to taste*

For Cauliflower Mash:

- *1 large head cauliflower, cut into florets*
- *2 tablespoons butter or olive oil*
- *2 cloves garlic, minced*
- *1/4 cup grated Parmesan cheese*
- *Salt and pepper to taste*
- *Chopped fresh parsley for garnish (optional)*

Instructions:

1. Preheat the oven to 400°F (200°C).

2. In a small bowl, whisk together lemon juice, lemon zest, minced garlic, olive oil, chopped rosemary, chopped thyme, salt, and pepper to create a marinade.

3. Place the chicken thighs in a large baking dish. Pour the marinade over the chicken thighs, ensuring they are evenly coated. Let them marinate for at least 15 minutes.

4. Arrange the chicken thighs skin-side up in the baking dish.

5. Roast in the preheated oven for about 30-35 minutes, or until the chicken is golden brown and cooked through, with an internal temperature of 165°F (74°C).

6. While the chicken is roasting, prepare the cauliflower mash. Steam or boil the cauliflower florets until they are tender, about 10-12 minutes. Drain well.

7. In a large bowl, combine the cooked cauliflower, minced garlic, butter or olive oil, grated Parmesan cheese, salt, and pepper. Mash the cauliflower using a potato masher or immersion blender until smooth and creamy.

8. Adjust seasoning to taste and keep warm until ready to serve.

9. Once the chicken thighs are done, remove them from the oven and let them rest for a few minutes.

10. Serve the lemon herb roasted chicken thighs hot with cauliflower mash.

11. Garnish with chopped fresh parsley if desired.

12. Enjoy your flavorful and comforting meal!

Nutritional Values (per serving):

- Calories: 350 kcal

- Carbohydrates: 10g

- Protein: 25g

- Fat: 25g

Glycemic Index: Low

7. Shrimp Stir-Fry with Snow Peas and Bell Peppers

Preparation Time: 15 minutes
Cooking Time: 10 minutes
Servings: 4

Ingredients:

- *1 lb medium shrimp, peeled and deveined*

- *2 cups snow peas, trimmed*

- *1 red bell pepper, thinly sliced*

- *1 yellow bell pepper, thinly sliced*

- *3 cloves garlic, minced*

- *1-inch piece ginger, minced*

- *2 tablespoons soy sauce (reduced-sodium if preferred)*

- *1 tablespoon oyster sauce*

- *1 tablespoon sesame oil*

- *1 tablespoon olive oil*

- *1 teaspoon cornstarch mixed with 2 tablespoons water*

- *Salt and pepper to taste*

- *Cooked rice or noodles for serving*

- *Sesame seeds for garnish (optional)*

- *Sliced green onions for garnish (optional)*

Instructions:

1. In a small bowl, mix together soy sauce, oyster sauce, sesame oil, minced garlic, minced ginger, and cornstarch slurry. Set aside.

2. Heat olive oil in a large skillet or wok over medium-high heat.

3. Add snow peas, red bell pepper, and yellow bell pepper to the skillet. Stir-fry for about 3-4 minutes until the vegetables are crisp-tender.

4. Push the vegetables to one side of the skillet and add the shrimp to the other side.

5. Cook the shrimp for 2-3 minutes on each side until they turn pink and opaque.

6. Stir the vegetables and shrimp together in the skillet.

7. Pour the sauce mixture over the shrimp and vegetables. Stir well to coat evenly.

8. Cook for an additional 1-2 minutes until the sauce thickens and coats the shrimp and vegetables.

9. Season with salt and pepper to taste.

10. Serve the shrimp stir-fry hot over cooked rice or noodles.

11. Garnish with sesame seeds and sliced green onions if desired.

12. Enjoy your flavorful and nutritious shrimp stir-fry!

Nutritional Values (per serving, without rice or noodles):

- Calories: 200 kcal
- Carbohydrates: 8g
- Protein: 25g
- Fat: 7g

Glycemic Index: Low

8. Eggplant Parmesan with Whole Wheat Pasta

Preparation Time: 20 minutes
Cooking Time: 40 minutes
Servings: 4

Ingredients:

- *1 large eggplant, sliced into 1/2-inch rounds*
- *2 eggs*
- *1 cup whole wheat breadcrumbs*
- *1/2 cup grated Parmesan cheese*

- *2 cups marinara sauce*
- *8 oz whole wheat pasta*
- *2 cups shredded mozzarella cheese*
- *Fresh basil leaves for garnish (optional)*
- *Salt and pepper to taste*
- *Olive oil for frying*

Instructions:

1. Preheat the oven to 375°F (190°C).

2. Cook the whole wheat pasta according to package instructions until al dente. Drain and set aside.

3. In a shallow dish, beat the eggs with a pinch of salt and pepper.

4. In another shallow dish, combine the whole wheat breadcrumbs with grated Parmesan cheese.

5. Dip each eggplant slice into the beaten eggs, then dredge in the breadcrumb mixture, pressing gently to adhere.

6. Heat olive oil in a large skillet over medium heat. Fry the breaded eggplant slices in batches until golden brown and crispy, about 3-4 minutes per side. Add more oil as needed. Place the fried eggplant slices on paper towels to drain excess oil.

7. Spread a thin layer of marinara sauce in the bottom of a baking dish.

8. Arrange a layer of fried eggplant slices over the sauce.

9. Spoon marinara sauce over the eggplant slices, then sprinkle with shredded mozzarella cheese.

10. Repeat the layers until all the eggplant slices are used, ending with a layer of marinara sauce and mozzarella cheese on top.

11. Cover the baking dish with aluminum foil and bake in the preheated oven for about 25-30 minutes, or until the cheese is melted and bubbly.

12. Remove the foil and bake for an additional 10 minutes to allow the cheese to brown slightly.

13. Serve the eggplant Parmesan hot over whole wheat pasta.

14. Garnish with fresh basil leaves if desired.

15. Enjoy your delicious and nutritious eggplant Parmesan with whole wheat pasta!

Nutritional Values (per serving):

- Calories: 450 kcal
- Carbohydrates: 50g
- Protein: 25g
- Fat: 18g

Glycemic Index: Medium

9. Beef and Vegetable Skewers with Quinoa

Preparation Time: 20 minutes
Cooking Time: 15 minutes
Servings: 4

Ingredients:

- *1 lb beef sirloin, cut into 1-inch cubes*
- *2 bell peppers (any color), cut into chunks*
- *1 large red onion, cut into chunks*
- *8-10 cherry tomatoes*
- *1 zucchini, sliced into rounds*
- *2 tablespoons olive oil*
- *2 cloves garlic, minced*
- *1 teaspoon dried oregano*
- *1 teaspoon paprika*
- *Salt and pepper to taste*
- *Wooden skewers, soaked in water for 30 minutes*

For Quinoa:

- *1 cup quinoa, rinsed*
- *2 cups water or vegetable broth*
- *Salt to taste*

Instructions:

1. In a bowl, combine olive oil, minced garlic, dried oregano, paprika, salt, and pepper. Mix well to create a marinade.

2. Add beef cubes to the marinade and toss until evenly coated. Allow to marinate for at least 15 minutes, or refrigerate for up to 2 hours.

3. Preheat the grill or grill pan over medium-high heat.

4. Thread marinated beef cubes onto skewers, alternating with bell pepper chunks, red onion chunks, cherry tomatoes, and zucchini rounds.

5. Grill the skewers for about 10-12 minutes, turning occasionally, until the beef is cooked to desired doneness and vegetables are tender and lightly charred.

6. While the skewers are cooking, rinse quinoa under cold water using a fine mesh strainer.

7. In a saucepan, bring water or vegetable broth to a boil. Add quinoa and a pinch of salt. Reduce heat to low, cover, and simmer for 15-20 minutes, or until quinoa is tender and water is absorbed. Remove from heat and let it sit covered for 5 minutes. Fluff with a fork.

8. Serve the beef and vegetable skewers hot with cooked quinoa.

9. Enjoy your nutritious and flavorful beef and vegetable skewers with quinoa!

Nutritional Values (per serving):

- Calories: 400 kcal

- Carbohydrates: 35g

- Protein: 30g

- Fat: 15g

Glycemic Index: Low

10.Mediterranean Chickpea Salad with Grilled Chicken

Preparation Time: 20 minutes
Cooking Time: 15 minutes
Servings: 4

Ingredients:

- *2 boneless, skinless chicken breasts*

- *1 can (15 oz) chickpeas, drained and rinsed*

- *1 cucumber, diced*

- *1 cup cherry tomatoes, halved*

- *1/2 red onion, thinly sliced*

- *1/4 cup Kalamata olives, pitted and sliced*

- *1/4 cup crumbled feta cheese*

- *1/4 cup chopped fresh parsley*

- *2 tablespoons extra virgin olive oil*

- *1 tablespoon red wine vinegar*

- *1 teaspoon dried oregano*

- *Salt and pepper to taste*

- *Lemon wedges for serving*

Instructions:

1. Preheat the grill or grill pan over medium-high heat.

2. Season the chicken breasts with salt, pepper, and dried oregano.

3. Grill the chicken breasts for about 6-8 minutes per side, or until cooked through and no longer pink in the center. Remove from the grill and let them rest for a few minutes before slicing.

4. In a large mixing bowl, combine the chickpeas, diced cucumber, cherry tomatoes, thinly sliced red onion, sliced Kalamata olives, crumbled feta cheese, and chopped fresh parsley.

5. In a small bowl, whisk together the extra virgin olive oil and red wine vinegar to make the dressing. Season with salt and pepper to taste.

6. Pour the dressing over the chickpea salad and toss gently to coat all the ingredients evenly.

7. Divide the chickpea salad among serving plates.

8. Slice the grilled chicken breasts and arrange them on top of the salad.

9. Serve the Mediterranean chickpea salad with grilled chicken immediately, garnished with lemon wedges.

10. Enjoy your refreshing and nutritious salad!

Nutritional Values (per serving):

- Calories: 350 kcal

- Carbohydrates: 25g

- Protein: 30g

- Fat: 15g

Glycemic Index: Low

11. Spinach and Mushroom Stuffed Chicken Breast

Preparation Time: 20 minutes
Cooking Time: 25 minutes
Servings: 4

Ingredients:

- *4 boneless, skinless chicken breasts*

- *2 cups fresh spinach leaves*

- *1 cup sliced mushrooms*

- *1/2 cup shredded mozzarella cheese*

- *2 cloves garlic, minced*

- *1 tablespoon olive oil*

- *1 teaspoon dried thyme*

- *1 teaspoon dried rosemary*

- *Salt and pepper to taste*
- *Toothpicks or kitchen twine for securing*

Instructions:

1. Preheat the oven to 375°F (190°C).

2. In a skillet, heat olive oil over medium heat. Add minced garlic and cook until fragrant, about 1 minute.

3. Add sliced mushrooms to the skillet and sauté until they release their moisture and become tender, about 5-7 minutes.

4. Add fresh spinach leaves to the skillet and cook until wilted, about 2-3 minutes.

5. Season the mushroom and spinach mixture with dried thyme, dried rosemary, salt, and pepper. Remove from heat and let it cool slightly.

6. Using a sharp knife, make a horizontal slit along the side of each chicken breast to create a pocket for the stuffing. Be careful not to cut all the way through.

7. Stuff each chicken breast with the mushroom and spinach mixture, then sprinkle shredded mozzarella cheese on top.

8. Secure the opening of each chicken breast with toothpicks or kitchen twine to keep the stuffing inside.

9. Season the outside of the chicken breasts with salt and pepper.

10. Heat a skillet over medium-high heat. Add olive oil.

11. Carefully place the stuffed chicken breasts in the skillet and sear them on both sides until golden brown, about 2-3 minutes per side.

12. Transfer the seared chicken breasts to a baking dish and bake in the preheated oven for about 15-20 minutes, or until the chicken is cooked through and no longer pink in the center.

13. Remove from the oven and let the chicken rest for a few minutes before serving.

14. Serve the spinach and mushroom stuffed chicken breasts hot.

15. Enjoy your flavorful and nutritious meal!

Nutritional Values (per serving):

- Calories: 250 kcal
- Carbohydrates: 4g
- Protein: 30g
- Fat: 12g

Glycemic Value: Low

12. Blackened Tilapia with Steamed Green Beans

Preparation Time: 10 minutes
Cooking Time: 10 minutes
Servings: 4

Ingredients:

- *4 tilapia fillets (about 6 oz each)*
- *1 tablespoon paprika*
- *1 teaspoon garlic powder*
- *1 teaspoon onion powder*
- *1 teaspoon dried thyme*
- *1 teaspoon dried oregano*
- *1/2 teaspoon cayenne pepper (adjust to taste)*
- *1/2 teaspoon black pepper*
- *1/2 teaspoon salt*
- *2 tablespoons olive oil*
- *1 lb fresh green beans, trimmed*
- *Lemon wedges for serving*

Instructions:

1. In a small bowl, combine paprika, garlic powder, onion powder, dried thyme, dried oregano, cayenne pepper, black pepper, and salt to create the blackening seasoning.

2. Pat dry the tilapia fillets with paper towels and rub both sides of each fillet with the blackening seasoning mixture.

3. Heat olive oil in a large skillet over medium-high heat.

4. Once the skillet is hot, add the tilapia fillets and cook for about 3-4 minutes on each side, or until the fish is cooked through and easily flakes with a fork. Adjust cooking time based on the thickness of the fillets.

5. While the tilapia is cooking, steam the green beans until tender-crisp, about 5-7 minutes.

6. Serve the blackened tilapia alongside the steamed green beans.

7. Garnish with lemon wedges.

8. Enjoy your flavorful and nutritious blackened tilapia with steamed green beans!

Nutritional Values (per serving):

- Calories: 200 kcal

- Carbohydrates:8g

- Protein: 25g

- Fat: 8g

Glycemic Value: Low

13. Cauliflower Fried Rice with Shrimp

Preparation Time: 15 minutes
Cooking Time: 15 minutes
Servings: 4

Ingredients:

- *1 medium head cauliflower, grated or finely chopped*

- *1 lb shrimp, peeled and deveined*

- *2 eggs, beaten*

- *1 cup mixed vegetables (such as carrots, peas, and bell peppers), diced*

- *4 green onions, chopped*

- *3 cloves garlic, minced*

- *2 tablespoons soy sauce (reduced-sodium if preferred)*

- *1 tablespoon sesame oil*

- *1 tablespoon olive oil*

- *Salt and pepper to taste*

- *Sesame seeds for garnish (optional)*

- *Sliced green onions for garnish (optional)*

Instructions:

1. In a large skillet or wok, heat olive oil over medium-high heat.

2. Add minced garlic and chopped green onions to the skillet. Sauté until fragrant, about 1 minute.

3. Add shrimp to the skillet and cook until pink and cooked through, about 2-3 minutes per side. Remove the shrimp from the skillet and set aside.

4. In the same skillet, push the vegetables to one side and pour the beaten eggs into the other side. Scramble the eggs until cooked through, then mix them with the vegetables.

5. Add the grated or finely chopped cauliflower to the skillet. Stir-fry for about 5-7 minutes until the cauliflower is tender and slightly golden.

6. Add cooked shrimp back to the skillet.

7. Pour soy sauce and sesame oil over the cauliflower and shrimp mixture. Stir well to combine and coat evenly.

8. Cook for an additional 2-3 minutes, allowing the flavors to meld together.

9. Season with salt and pepper to taste.

10. Remove from heat and garnish with sesame seeds and sliced green onions if desired.

11. Serve the cauliflower fried rice with shrimp hot.

12. Enjoy your delicious and healthy cauliflower fried rice with shrimp!

Nutritional Values (per serving):

- Calories: 250 kcal

- Carbohydrates: 10g

- Protein: 25g

- Fat: 12g

Glycemic Value: Low

14. Greek Turkey Burgers with Greek Salad

Preparation Time: 20 minutes
Cooking Time: 15 minutes
Servings: 4

Ingredients:

For Greek Turkey Burgers:

- *1 lb ground turkey*

- *1/2 cup crumbled feta cheese*

- *1/4 cup chopped fresh parsley*

- *1/4 cup finely chopped red onion*

- *2 cloves garlic, minced*

- *1 teaspoon dried oregano*

- *1 teaspoon dried basil*

- *Salt and pepper to taste*

- *Olive oil for cooking*

For Greek Salad:

- *2 large tomatoes, diced*

- *1 cucumber, diced*

- *1/2 red onion, thinly sliced*
- *1/2 cup Kalamata olives, pitted*
- *1/2 cup crumbled feta cheese*
- *2 tablespoons extra virgin olive oil*
- *1 tablespoon red wine vinegar*
- *1 teaspoon dried oregano*
- *Salt and pepper to taste*
- *Fresh parsley for garnish (optional)*
- *Whole wheat burger buns for serving (optional)*

Instructions:

1. In a large mixing bowl, combine ground turkey, crumbled feta cheese, chopped parsley, chopped red onion, minced garlic, dried oregano, dried basil, salt, and pepper. Mix until well combined.

2. Divide the turkey mixture into 4 equal portions and shape them into burger patties.

3. Heat olive oil in a skillet or grill pan over medium heat.

4. Cook the turkey burgers for about 6-7 minutes on each side, or until cooked through and browned on the outside.

5. While the burgers are cooking, prepare the Greek salad. In a large bowl, combine diced tomatoes, diced cucumber, thinly sliced red onion, Kalamata olives, and crumbled feta cheese.

6. In a small bowl, whisk together extra virgin olive oil, red wine vinegar, dried oregano, salt, and pepper to make the salad dressing.

7. Pour the dressing over the salad and toss gently to coat all the ingredients evenly.

8. To serve, place a turkey burger on a whole wheat bun (if using) and top with a generous portion of Greek salad.

9. Garnish with fresh parsley if desired.

10. Serve the Greek turkey burgers with Greek salad immediately.

11. Enjoy your delicious and nutritious meal!

Nutritional Values (per serving, without bun):

- Calories: 350 kcal
- Carbohydrates: 10g
- Protein: 30g
- Fat: 20g

Glycemic Value: Low

15. Lentil Soup with Spinach and Tomatoes

Preparation Time: 15 minutes
Cooking Time: 30 minutes
Servings: 6

Ingredients:

- *1 cup dried green or brown lentils, rinsed and drained*
- *1 onion, finely chopped*
- *3 cloves garlic, minced*
- *2 carrots, diced*
- *2 celery stalks, diced*
- *1 can (14.5 oz) diced tomatoes*
- *4 cups vegetable broth*
- *2 cups fresh spinach leaves, chopped*
- *2 tablespoons olive oil*
- *1 teaspoon dried thyme*
- *1 teaspoon dried oregano*
- *Salt and pepper to taste*
- *Lemon wedges for serving (optional)*
- *Fresh parsley for garnish (optional)*

Instructions:

1. In a large pot, heat olive oil over medium heat.
2. Add chopped onion and minced garlic to the pot. Sauté until softened and fragrant, about 3-4 minutes.
3. Add diced carrots and celery to the pot. Cook for another 3-4 minutes until the vegetables start to soften.
4. Stir in dried thyme and dried oregano. Cook for another minute to release the flavors.
5. Add rinsed lentils, diced tomatoes (with their juices), and vegetable broth to the pot. Stir to combine.
6. Bring the soup to a boil, then reduce heat to low and let it simmer, covered, for about 20-25 minutes or until the lentils are tender.
7. Once the lentils are cooked, stir in the chopped spinach leaves and cook for an additional 2-3 minutes until the spinach wilts.
8. Season the soup with salt and pepper to taste.
9. Remove the pot from the heat and let the soup cool slightly before serving.

10. Ladle the lentil soup into bowls and garnish with fresh parsley if desired.

11. Serve hot with lemon wedges on the side for squeezing over the soup, if desired.

12. Enjoy your hearty and nutritious lentil soup with spinach and tomatoes!

Nutritional Values (per serving):

- Calories: 180 kcal

- Carbohydrates: 30g

- Protein: 10g

- Fat: 3g

- Fiber: 8g

Glycemic Value: Low

1. Greek Yogurt with Berries

Preparation Time: 5 minutes
Cooking Time: 0 minutes
Servings: 1

Ingredients:

- *1/2 cup Greek yogurt*
- *1/2 cup mixed berries (such as strawberries, blueberries, raspberries)*
- *1 teaspoon honey or stevia (optional, to taste)*
- *Fresh mint leaves for garnish (optional)*

Instructions:

1. Wash the berries thoroughly under cold water and pat them dry with a paper towel.
2. In a serving bowl or glass, spoon the Greek yogurt.
3. Top the Greek yogurt with the mixed berries.
4. Drizzle honey or sprinkle stevia over the berries if desired, adjusting to your taste preferences.
5. Garnish with fresh mint leaves for added freshness and flavor.
6. Serve immediately and enjoy your nutritious Greek yogurt with berries!

Nutritional Values (per serving):

- Calories: 150 kcal
- Carbohydrates: 20g
- Protein: 12g
- Fat: 2g
- Fiber: 5g

Glycemic Value: Low

2. Cucumber Slices with Hummus

Preparation Time: 10 minutes
Cooking Time: 0 minutes
Servings: 4

Ingredients:

- *2 large cucumbers*

- *1 cup hummus (store-bought or homemade)*

- *Fresh parsley or dill for garnish (optional)*

- *Lemon wedges for serving (optional)*

Instructions:

1. Wash the cucumbers thoroughly under cold water and pat them dry with a paper towel.

2. Slice the cucumbers into thin rounds, about 1/4 inch thick.

3. Arrange the cucumber slices on a serving platter or plate.

4. Place the hummus in a small bowl in the center of the serving platter.

5. Garnish the hummus with fresh parsley or dill if desired.

6. Serve the cucumber slices with hummus and lemon wedges on the side for squeezing over the cucumber slices.

7. Enjoy your refreshing and nutritious snack!

Nutritional Values (per serving):

- Calories: 100 kcal

- Carbohydrates: 10g

- Protein: 5g

- Fat: 5g

- Fiber: 5g

Glycemic Value: Low

3. Hard-Boiled Eggs

Preparation Time: 2 minutes
Cooking Time: 10-12 minutes
Servings: Variable

Ingredients:

- *Eggs (as many as desired)*

Instructions:

1. Place the eggs in a single layer in a saucepan or pot.

2. Fill the saucepan with enough cold water to cover the eggs by about 1 inch.

3. Place the saucepan on the stove over high heat and bring the water to a boil.

4. Once the water reaches a rolling boil, remove the saucepan from the heat.

5. Cover the saucepan with a lid and let the eggs sit in the hot water for about 10-12 minutes for hard-boiled eggs.

6. While the eggs are cooking, prepare a bowl of ice water.

7. After the eggs have finished cooking, carefully transfer them to the bowl of ice water using a slotted spoon.

8. Let the eggs sit in the ice water bath for a few minutes to cool down and stop the cooking process.

9. Once the eggs are cool, gently tap them on a hard surface to crack the shells, then peel off the shells under cold running water.

10. Pat the peeled eggs dry with a paper towel.

11. Hard-boiled eggs can be served immediately, or they can be stored in the refrigerator for up to one week.

Nutritional Values (per large egg):

- Calories: 70 kcal

- Protein:6g

- Fat: 5g

- Carbohydrates: 0g

- Fiber: 0g

Glycemic Value: Low

4. Apple Slices with Almond Butter

Preparation Time: 5 minutes
Cooking Time: 0 minutes
Servings: 2

Ingredients:

- *1 large apple (such as Honeycrisp or Fuji)*
- *4 tablespoons almond butter*

Instructions:

1. Wash the apple thoroughly under cold water and pat it dry with a paper towel.
2. Core the apple and slice it into thin wedges or rounds.
3. Arrange the apple slices on a serving plate or platter.
4. Place almond butter in a small bowl for dipping or spread it onto the apple slices directly.
5. Serve the apple slices with almond butter immediately.

Nutritional Values (per serving):

- Calories: 250 kcal
- Carbohydrates: 20g
- Protein: 7g
- Fat: 18g
- Fiber: 6g

Glycemic Value: Medium (due to natural sugars in the apple)

5. Celery Sticks with Cream Cheese

Preparation Time: 10 minutes
Cooking Time: 0 minutes
Servings: 4

Ingredients:

- *4 stalks of celery*
- *4 tablespoons cream cheese (softened)*
- *Optional toppings: Everything bagel seasoning, chopped chives, paprika*

Instructions:

1. Wash the celery stalks thoroughly under cold water and pat them dry with a paper towel.
2. Cut the celery stalks into manageable sticks, about 4 inches long.
3. Spread softened cream cheese onto one side of each celery stick.
4. If desired, sprinkle optional toppings like everything bagel seasoning, chopped chives, or paprika over the cream cheese.
5. Arrange the celery sticks on a serving plate or platter.
6. Serve immediately and enjoy your delicious celery sticks with cream cheese!

Nutritional Values (per serving):

- Calories: 70 kcal
- Carbohydrates: 2g
- Protein: 2g
- Fat: 6g
- Fiber: 1g

Glycemic Value: Low

6. Mixed Nuts and Seeds

Preparation Time: 5 minutes
Cooking Time: 0 minutes
Servings: 4

Ingredients:

- *1/2 cup almonds*
- *1/2 cup walnuts*
- *1/4 cup pumpkin seeds (pepitas)*
- *1/4 cup sunflower seeds*
- *1/4 cup cashews*
- *1/4 cup pecans*
- *1/4 teaspoon salt (optional)*

Instructions:

1. In a large mixing bowl, combine all the nuts and seeds.
2. If desired, sprinkle with salt and toss gently to distribute evenly.
3. Store the mixed nuts and seeds in an airtight container.

Nutritional Values (per serving, about 1/4 cup):

- Calories: 200 kcal
- Carbohydrates: 5g
- Protein: 7g
- Fat: 18g
- Fiber: 3g

Glycemic Value: Low

7. Cheese Cubes and Cherry Tomatoes

Preparation Time: 5 minutes
Cooking Time: 0 minutes
Servings: 4

Ingredients:

- *8 ounces cheese (such as cheddar, mozzarella, or pepper jack), cut into cubes*

- *1 pint cherry tomatoes*

- *Toothpicks (optional, for serving)*

Instructions:

1. Wash the cherry tomatoes thoroughly under cold water and pat them dry with a paper towel.

2. Cut the cheese into cubes, about 1 inch in size.

3. If desired, skewer one cheese cube followed by one cherry tomato onto each toothpick.

4. Arrange the cheese cubes and cherry tomatoes on a serving platter.

5. Serve immediately.

Nutritional Values (per serving):

- Calories:150 kcal

- Carbohydrates: 5g

- Protein: 9g

- Fat: 10g

- Fiber: 1g

Glycemic Value: Low

8. Avocado Slices with Lime and Sea Salt

Preparation Time: 5 minutes
Cooking Time: 0 minutes
Servings: 2

Ingredients:

- *1 ripe avocado*
- *1 lime*
- *Sea salt, to taste*

Instructions:

1. Cut the avocado in half lengthwise and remove the pit.
2. Carefully slice the avocado halves lengthwise into thin slices.
3. Arrange the avocado slices on a serving plate or platter.
4. Cut the lime in half and squeeze the juice over the avocado slices.
5. Sprinkle sea salt over the avocado slices to taste.
6. Serve immediately.

Nutritional Values (per serving):

- Calories: 160 kcal
- Carbohydrates: 9g
- Protein: 2g
- Fat: 15g
- Fiber:7g

Glycemic Value: Low

9. Whole Grain Crackers with Tuna Salad

Preparation Time: 10 minutes
Cooking Time: 0 minutes
Servings: 4

Ingredients:

- *1 can (5 oz) tuna, drained*
- *2 tablespoons mayonnaise*
- *1 tablespoon lemon juice*
- *1 stalk celery, finely chopped*
- *2 tablespoons red onion, finely chopped*
- *1 tablespoon fresh parsley, chopped*
- *Salt and pepper, to taste*
- *Whole grain crackers, for serving*

Instructions:

1. In a mixing bowl, combine the drained tuna, mayonnaise, lemon juice, chopped celery, chopped red onion, and chopped parsley.
2. Mix well until all ingredients are evenly incorporated.
3. Season the tuna salad with salt and pepper to taste. Adjust seasoning as needed.
4. Arrange whole grain crackers on a serving plate.
5. Spoon a portion of the tuna salad onto each cracker.
6. Garnish with additional parsley, if desired.
7. Serve immediately.

Nutritional Values (per serving, excluding crackers):

- Calories: 90 kcal
- Carbohydrates: 2g
- Protein: 8g
- Fat: 5g
- Fiber: 0.5g

Glycemic Value: Low

10. Carrot Sticks with Guacamole

Preparation Time: 10 minutes
Cooking Time: 0 minutes
Servings: 4

Ingredients:

- *4 large carrots, peeled and cut into sticks*
- *2 ripe avocados*
- *1 lime, juiced*
- *1/4 cup red onion, finely diced*
- *1/4 cup tomato, diced*
- *1/4 cup cilantro, chopped*
- *Salt and pepper, to taste*

Instructions:

1. Peel the carrots and cut them into sticks. Set aside.
2. Cut the avocados in half, remove the pits, and scoop the flesh into a mixing bowl.
3. Mash the avocado with a fork until smooth.
4. Add lime juice to the mashed avocado and mix well to combine.
5. Stir in the diced red onion, diced tomato, and chopped cilantro into the avocado mixture.
6. Season the guacamole with salt and pepper to taste. Adjust seasoning as needed.
7. Place the guacamole in a serving bowl.
8. Arrange the carrot sticks on a serving plate.
9. Serve the carrot sticks with the guacamole.
10. Enjoy your healthy and delicious snack!

Nutritional Values (per serving, guacamole only):

- Calories: 120 kcal
- Carbohydrates: 7g
- Protein: 2g
- Fat: 11g
- Fiber: 5g

Glycemic Value: Low

11. Edamame Beans

Preparation Time: 5 minutes
Cooking Time: 5 minutes
Servings: 4

Ingredients:

- *2 cups frozen edamame beans (in pods)*

- *Water for boiling*

- *Salt (optional), for seasoning*

Instructions:

1. Bring a pot of water to a boil.

2. Add the frozen edamame beans (in pods) to the boiling water.

3. Boil the edamame beans for about 4-5 minutes, or until they are tender.

4. Drain the cooked edamame beans and rinse them under cold water to stop the cooking process.

5. Pat the edamame beans dry with a paper towel.

6. Season the edamame beans with salt if desired.

7. Serve the edamame beans in a bowl.

8. Enjoy them as a healthy and nutritious snack!

Nutritional Values (per serving, about 1/2 cup):

- Calories: 120 kcal

- Carbohydrates: 9g

- Protein: 11g

- Fat: 4.5g

- Fiber: 5g

Glycemic Value: Low

12. Sliced Bell Peppers with Cottage Cheese

Preparation Time: 10 minutes
Cooking Time: 0 minutes
Servings: 2

Ingredients:

- *2 large bell peppers (any color), sliced*
- *1 cup cottage cheese*
- *Salt and pepper, to taste*
- *Optional: Fresh herbs (such as parsley or chives) for garnish*

Instructions:

1. Wash the bell peppers thoroughly under cold water. Remove the stems and seeds, then slice them into strips.
2. Place the cottage cheese in a bowl and season it with salt and pepper according to taste.
3. Arrange the sliced bell peppers on a serving plate.
4. Serve the cottage cheese alongside the sliced bell peppers.
5. Optionally, garnish with fresh herbs before serving.

Nutritional Values (per serving):

- Calories: 120 kcal
- Carbohydrates: 10g
- Protein: 12g
- Fat: 4g
- Fiber: 3g

Glycemic Value: Low

13. Turkey Roll-Ups with Lettuce and Mustard

Preparation Time: 10 minutes
Cooking Time: 0 minutes
Servings: 2

Ingredients:

- *6 slices of turkey breast (about 4 ounces)*

- *2 large lettuce leaves*

- *2 tablespoons mustard*

- *Salt and pepper, to taste*

Instructions:

1. Lay out the turkey slices on a clean surface.

2. Spread mustard evenly over each turkey slice.

3. Place a lettuce leaf on top of each turkey slice.

4. Season with salt and pepper to taste.

5. Roll up each turkey slice with the lettuce inside.

6. Secure each roll-up with a toothpick if desired.

7. Serve immediately or refrigerate until ready to eat.

Nutritional Values (per serving):

- Calories: 100 kcal

- Carbohydrates: 2g

- Protein: 15g

- Fat: 3g

- Fiber: 1g

Glycemic Value: Low

14.Sugar-Free Jello with Whipped Cream

Preparation Time: 5 minutes
Cooking Time: 0 minutes
Chilling Time: 2 hours
Servings: 4

Ingredients:

- *1 package (0.3 oz) sugar-free flavored gelatin (any flavor of your choice)*

- *1 cup boiling water*

- *1 cup cold water*

- *1/2 cup heavy whipping cream*

- *1 tablespoon powdered erythritol (or any preferred sugar substitute)*

- *Optional: Fresh berries for garnish*

Instructions:

1. In a mixing bowl, add the sugar-free flavored gelatin powder.

2. Pour boiling water over the gelatin powder and stir until completely dissolved.

3. Add cold water to the gelatin mixture and stir to combine.

4. Pour the gelatin mixture into individual serving cups or a large serving bowl.

5. Refrigerate the gelatin for at least 2 hours, or until set.

6. In a separate mixing bowl, whip the heavy whipping cream and powdered erythritol together until stiff peaks form.

7. Once the gelatin has set, remove it from the refrigerator.

8. Top each serving of sugar-free Jello with a dollop of whipped cream.

9. Garnish with fresh berries, if desired.

10. Serve chilled and enjoy your sugar-free treat!

Nutritional Values (per serving):

- Calories: 70 kcal

- Carbohydrates: 1g

- Protein: 1g

- Fat: 7g

- Fiber: 0g

Glycemic Value: Low

15. Homemade Trail Mix

Preparation Time: 5 minutes
Cooking Time: 0 minutes
Servings: 8

Ingredients:

- *1 cup raw almonds*
- *1 cup raw cashews*
- *1 cup roasted peanuts (unsalted)*
- *1 cup dried cranberries*
- *1/2 cup dark chocolate chips*
- *1/2 cup raisins*
- *1/2 cup pumpkin seeds*
- *1/2 cup sunflower seeds*
- *Optional: 1/2 teaspoon sea salt (if using unsalted nuts)*

Instructions:

1. In a large mixing bowl, combine all the ingredients.
2. If using unsalted nuts and seeds, add sea salt to taste.
3. Mix well until all ingredients are evenly distributed.
4. Transfer the trail mix to an airtight container or individual snack bags for storage.
5. Store in a cool, dry place or refrigerate if desired.

Nutritional Values (per serving, about 1/4 cup):

- Calories: 220 kcal
- Carbohydrates: 5g
- Protein: 8g
- Fat: 15g
- Fiber: 3g

Glycemic Value: Medium (due to dried fruits and chocolate chips)

Desserts

1. Sugar-Free Berry Parfait

Preparation Time: 15 minutes
Cooking Time: 0 minutes
Servings: 2

Ingredients:

- *1 cup fresh mixed berries (such as strawberries, blueberries, raspberries)*
- *1 cup sugar-free Greek yogurt*
- *1/4 cup sugar-free granola*
- *1 tablespoon sugar-free honey or sugar substitute (optional)*
- *Fresh mint leaves for garnish (optional)*

Instructions:

1. Wash the berries thoroughly and pat them dry with paper towels. Slice the strawberries if they are large.
2. In a bowl, mix the sugar-free Greek yogurt with the sugar-free honey or sugar substitute, if using.
3. In serving glasses or bowls, layer the sugar-free Greek yogurt, followed by a layer of mixed berries.
4. Repeat the layers until the glasses are almost full, ending with a layer of berries on top.
5. Sprinkle the sugar-free granola over the top layer of berries.
6. Garnish with fresh mint leaves, if desired.
7. Serve immediately or refrigerate until ready to serve.

Nutritional Values (per serving):

- Calories: 120 kcal
- Carbohydrates: 15g
- Protein: 8g
- Fat: 3g
- Fiber: 5g

Glycemic Value: Low

2. Dark Chocolate Avocado Mousse

Preparation Time: 15 minutes
Cooking Time: 0 minutes
Servings: 4

Ingredients:

- *2 ripe avocados, peeled and pitted*
- *1/4 cup unsweetened cocoa powder*
- *1/4 cup sugar-free maple syrup or sweetener of choice*
- *1 teaspoon vanilla extract*
- *1/4 cup unsweetened almond milk (or any milk of choice)*
- *Pinch of salt*
- *Optional toppings: fresh berries, chopped nuts, whipped cream (sugar-free)*

Instructions:

1. In a food processor or blender, combine the ripe avocados, unsweetened cocoa powder, sugar-free maple syrup, vanilla extract, almond milk, and a pinch of salt.

2. Blend the ingredients until smooth and creamy, scraping down the sides of the blender or food processor as needed.

3. Taste the mousse and adjust the sweetness or cocoa powder according to your preference.

4. Once the mousse reaches your desired consistency and taste, transfer it to serving bowls or glasses.

5. Cover the mousse with plastic wrap and refrigerate for at least 1 hour to chill and set.

6. Before serving, garnish the mousse with fresh berries, chopped nuts, or a dollop of sugar-free whipped cream, if desired.

Nutritional Values (per serving):

- Calories: 150 kcal
- Carbohydrates: 10g
- Protein: 2g
- Fat: 12g
- Fiber: 6g

Glycemic Value: Low

3. Greek Yogurt Popsicles

Preparation Time: 10 minutes
Freezing Time: 4-6 hours
Servings: Makes 6 popsicles

Ingredients:

- *2 cups Greek yogurt (plain, unsweetened)*
- *1 cup mixed berries (such as strawberries, blueberries, raspberries)*
- *2 tablespoons honey or maple syrup (optional)*
- *1 teaspoon vanilla extract (optional)*
- *Popsicle molds*
- *Popsicle sticks*

Instructions:

1. In a mixing bowl, combine Greek yogurt with honey or maple syrup and vanilla extract (if using). Stir until the mixture is well combined and smooth.

2. Wash the mixed berries thoroughly under running water. Pat them dry with a paper towel, then chop them into small pieces.

3. Divide the chopped berries evenly among the popsicle molds.

4. Pour the Greek yogurt mixture over the berries in the molds, filling each mold to the top.

5. Insert the popsicle sticks into the center of each mold, ensuring they are standing upright.

6. Gently tap the molds on the counter to remove any air bubbles and to level the mixture.

7. Place the popsicle molds in the freezer and let them freeze for at least 4-6 hours, or until completely solid.

8. Once the popsicles are frozen, remove them from the molds by running warm water over the outsides of the molds for a few seconds.

9. Serve the Greek yogurt popsicles immediately and enjoy the refreshing treat!

Nutritional Information (per serving, based on 1 popsicle):

- Calories: 80 kcal
- Carbohydrates: 12g
- Protein: 6g
- Fat: 0g
- Fiber: 2g

Glycemic Value: Low

4. Almond Flour Lemon Cake

Preparation Time: 15 minutes
Cooking Time: 30-35 minutes
Servings: 8-10

Ingredients:

- *2 cups almond flour*
- *1/2 cup granulated erythritol or sweetener of choice*
- *1 teaspoon baking powder*
- *1/4 teaspoon salt*
- *3 large eggs*
- *1/4 cup unsweetened almond milk (or any milk of choice)*
- *Zest of 2 lemons*
- *Juice of 1 lemon*
- *1/4 cup melted coconut oil or butter*
- *1 teaspoon vanilla extract*
- *Optional: powdered erythritol for dusting*

Instructions:

1. Preheat your oven to 350°F (175°C). Grease an 8-inch round cake pan and line the bottom with parchment paper.

2. In a large mixing bowl, whisk together the almond flour, granulated erythritol, baking powder, and salt until well combined.

3. In another bowl, beat the eggs with almond milk, lemon zest, lemon juice, melted coconut oil or butter, and vanilla extract until smooth.

4. Gradually add the wet ingredients to the dry ingredients, stirring until a smooth batter forms.

5. Pour the batter into the prepared cake pan and spread it evenly.

6. Bake in the preheated oven for 30-35 minutes, or until the top is golden brown and a toothpick inserted into the center comes out clean.

7. Remove the cake from the oven and let it cool in the pan for 10 minutes.

8. Carefully transfer the cake to a wire rack to cool completely.

9. Once cooled, dust the top of the cake with powdered erythritol, if desired.

10. Slice and serve the almond flour lemon cake.

Nutritional Information (per serving, based on 1 slice, assuming 10 servings):

- Calories: 200 kcal

- Carbohydrates: 6g

- Protein: 7g

- Fat: 17g

- Fiber: 3g

Glycemic Value: Low

5. Chia Seed Pudding with Berries

Preparation Time: 5 minutes
Chilling Time: 4 hours or overnight
Servings: 2

Ingredients:

- *1/4 cup chia seeds*

- *1 cup unsweetened almond milk (or any milk of choice)*

- *1 tablespoon honey or maple syrup (optional, for sweetness)*

- *1/2 teaspoon vanilla extract*

- *1/2 cup mixed berries (such as strawberries, blueberries, raspberries)*

- *Fresh mint leaves for garnish (optional)*

Instructions:

1. In a mixing bowl, combine the chia seeds, unsweetened almond milk, honey or maple syrup (if using), and vanilla extract.

2. Stir the mixture well until the chia seeds are evenly distributed.

3. Let the mixture sit for about 5 minutes, then stir again to prevent clumping.

4. Cover the bowl and refrigerate the chia seed mixture for at least 4 hours or overnight, allowing it to thicken.

5. Once the chia pudding has set, give it a good stir to break up any clumps.

6. Divide the chia seed pudding into serving bowls or jars.

7. Top each serving with mixed berries.

8. Garnish with fresh mint leaves, if desired.

9. Serve chilled and enjoy!

Nutritional Information (per serving):

- Calories: 150 kcal

- Carbohydrates: 18g

- Protein: 4g

- Fat: 7g

- Fiber 10g

Glycemic Value: Low

6. Coconut Flour Chocolate Chip Cookies

Preparation Time: 15 minutes
Cooking Time: 10-12 minutes
Servings: Makes about 12 cookies

Ingredients:

- *1/2 cup coconut flour*

- *1/2 teaspoon baking soda*

- *1/4 teaspoon salt*

- *1/4 cup coconut oil, melted*

- *1/4 cup honey or maple syrup*

- *2 large eggs*

- *1 teaspoon vanilla extract*

- *1/3 cup dark chocolate chips (sugar-free if desired)*

Instructions:

1. Preheat your oven to 350°F (175°C). Line a baking sheet with parchment paper or silicone baking mats.

2. In a medium-sized mixing bowl, whisk together the coconut flour, baking soda, and salt until well combined.

3. In a separate large mixing bowl, whisk together the melted coconut oil, honey or maple syrup, eggs, and vanilla extract until smooth.

4. Gradually add the dry ingredients to the wet ingredients, stirring until a dough forms.

5. Fold in the dark chocolate chips until evenly distributed throughout the dough.

6. Allow the dough to sit for a few minutes to let the coconut flour absorb some moisture.

7. Using a spoon or cookie scoop, drop rounded tablespoons of dough onto the prepared baking sheet, spacing them about 2 inches apart.

8. Use your fingers or the back of a spoon to gently flatten each cookie dough mound.

9. Bake in the preheated oven for 10-12 minutes, or until the edges are golden brown.

10. Remove from the oven and let the cookies cool on the baking sheet for 5 minutes before transferring them to a wire rack to cool completely.

11. Once cooled, store the cookies in an airtight container at room temperature for up to 5 days.

Nutritional Information (per cookie):

- Calories: 100 kcal

- Carbohydrates: 9g

- Protein: 2g

- Fat: 7g

- Fiber: 2g

Glycemic Value: Low

7. Sugar-Free Apple Crisp

Preparation Time: 15 minutes
Cooking Time: 35-40 minutes
Servings: 6

Ingredients:

- *4 medium-sized apples, peeled, cored, and thinly sliced*

- *1 tablespoon lemon juice*

- *1 teaspoon ground cinnamon*

- *1/2 teaspoon ground nutmeg*

- *1/4 cup water*

- *1 cup old-fashioned rolled oats*

- *1/2 cup almond flour*

- *1/4 cup chopped walnuts or pecans*

- *1/4 cup melted coconut oil*

- *2 tablespoons sugar-free maple syrup or sweetener of choice*

- *Pinch of salt*

Instructions:

1. Preheat your oven to 350°F (175°C). Grease a baking dish with coconut oil or non-stick spray.

2. In a large mixing bowl, combine the sliced apples, lemon juice, cinnamon, nutmeg, and water. Toss until the apples are evenly coated with the spices and lemon juice.

3. In a separate mixing bowl, combine the rolled oats, almond flour, chopped nuts, melted coconut oil, sugar-free maple syrup, and a pinch of salt. Mix until well combined and crumbly.

4. Spread the coated apple slices evenly in the prepared baking dish.

5. Sprinkle the oat and nut mixture evenly over the top of the apples.

6. Bake in the preheated oven for 35-40 minutes, or until the topping is golden brown and the apples are tender.

7. Remove from the oven and let it cool for a few minutes before serving.

8. Serve warm, optionally with a dollop of sugar-free whipped cream or a scoop of sugar-free vanilla ice cream.

Nutritional Information (per serving):

- Calories: 200 kcal

- Carbohydrates: 25g

- Protein: 4g

- Fat: 10g

- Fiber: 5g

Glycemic Value: Low

8. Baked Cinnamon Apples

Preparation Time: 10 minutes
Cooking Time: 30 minutes
Servings: 4

Ingredients:

- *4 large apples (such as Granny Smith or Honeycrisp), cored and sliced*

- *2 tablespoons unsalted butter, melted*

- *2 tablespoons honey or maple syrup*

- *1 teaspoon ground cinnamon*

- *1/4 teaspoon ground nutmeg*

- *1/4 cup water*

- *Optional: whipped cream or vanilla ice cream for serving*

Instructions:

1. Preheat your oven to 375°F (190°C). Grease a baking dish with butter or cooking spray.

2. In a small bowl, mix together the melted butter, honey or maple syrup, ground cinnamon, and ground nutmeg until well combined.

3. Place the sliced apples in the greased baking dish, arranging them in a single layer.

4. Drizzle the honey-butter mixture over the sliced apples.

5. Pour the water into the bottom of the baking dish to prevent the apples from drying out during baking.

6. Cover the baking dish with aluminum foil and bake in the preheated oven for 20 minutes.

7. After 20 minutes, remove the foil and continue baking for an additional 10 minutes, or until the apples are tender and lightly caramelized.

8. Remove from the oven and let the baked cinnamon apples cool slightly before serving.

9. Serve warm as is or with a dollop of whipped cream or a scoop of vanilla ice cream, if desired.

Nutritional Information (per serving):

- Calories: 140 kcal

- Carbohydrates: 30g

- Protein: 1g

- Fat: 3g

- Fiber: 5g

Glycemic Value: Moderate

9. Low-Carb Cheesecake Bites

Preparation Time: 20 minutes
Chilling Time: 2 hours
Servings: Makes about 12 cheesecake bites

Ingredients:

- *1 cup almond flour*

- *3 tablespoons powdered erythritol or sweetener of choice*

- *3 tablespoons unsalted butter, melted*

- *8 ounces cream cheese, softened*

- *1/4 cup powdered erythritol or sweetener of choice*

- *1 teaspoon vanilla extract*

- *1/4 cup heavy cream*

- *Fresh berries or sugar-free fruit topping (optional)*

Instructions:

1. In a mixing bowl, combine the almond flour, 3 tablespoons of powdered erythritol, and melted butter. Mix until well combined and the mixture resembles coarse crumbs.

2. Line a mini muffin pan with paper liners or silicone molds.

3. Press about a tablespoon of the almond flour mixture firmly into the bottom of each muffin cup to form the crust. Use the back of a spoon to press it down evenly.

4. In a separate mixing bowl, beat the softened cream cheese, 1/4 cup powdered erythritol, and vanilla extract until smooth and creamy.

5. In another bowl, whip the heavy cream until stiff peaks form.

6. Gently fold the whipped cream into the cream cheese mixture until well combined.

7. Spoon the cream cheese mixture evenly over the almond flour crusts in the muffin pan.

8. Smooth the tops with a spatula or the back of a spoon.

9. Cover the muffin pan with plastic wrap and refrigerate for at least 2 hours, or until the cheesecake bites are set.

10. Once set, remove the cheesecake bites from the muffin pan and transfer them to a serving plate.

11. If desired, top each cheesecake bite with fresh berries or sugar-free fruit topping before serving.

Nutritional Information (per serving - 1 cheesecake bite):

- Calories: 130 kcal
- Carbohydrates: 2g
- Protein: 2g
- Fat: 13g
- Fiber: 1g

Glycemic Value: Low

10. Avocado Chocolate Pudding

Preparation Time: 10 minutes
Chilling Time: 1 hour
Servings: Makes 4 servings

Ingredients:

- *2 ripe avocados, peeled and pitted*
- *1/4 cup unsweetened cocoa powder*
- *1/4 cup honey or maple syrup*

- *1 teaspoon vanilla extract*

- *1/4 cup almond milk or any milk of choice*

- *Pinch of salt*

- *Optional toppings: sliced strawberries, raspberries, or whipped cream*

Instructions:

1. In a food processor or blender, combine the ripe avocados, unsweetened cocoa powder, honey or maple syrup, vanilla extract, almond milk, and a pinch of salt.

2. Blend until the mixture is smooth and creamy, scraping down the sides of the blender or food processor as needed.

3. Taste the pudding and adjust the sweetness or cocoa powder according to your preference.

4. Once the pudding is smooth and well combined, transfer it to a bowl or individual serving dishes.

5. Cover the pudding with plastic wrap, ensuring that the plastic wrap is touching the surface of the pudding to prevent it from forming a skin.

6. Refrigerate the pudding for at least 1 hour to chill and firm up.

7. Before serving, garnish the pudding with sliced strawberries, raspberries, or a dollop of whipped cream if desired.

Nutritional Information (per serving):

- Calories: 180 kcal

- Carbohydrates: 20g

- Protein: 2g

- Fat: 12g

- Fiber: 7g

Glycemic Value: Low

11. Walnut and Date Energy Balls

Preparation Time: 15 minutes
Cooking Time: 0 minutes
Servings: Makes about 12 energy balls

Ingredients:

- *1 cup walnuts*

- *1 cup pitted dates*

- *2 tablespoons unsweetened cocoa powder*

- *1 tablespoon honey or maple syrup (optional, adjust to taste)*

- *1 teaspoon vanilla extract*

- *Pinch of salt*

- *Shredded coconut or cocoa powder for coating (optional)*

Instructions:

1. In a food processor, add the walnuts, pitted dates, unsweetened cocoa powder, honey or maple syrup (if using), vanilla extract, and a pinch of salt.

2. Process the mixture until it forms a sticky dough-like consistency and the ingredients are well combined. Stop and scrape down the sides of the food processor as needed.

3. Once the mixture is ready, take about 1 tablespoon of the mixture and roll it between your palms to form a ball. Repeat with the remaining mixture to make more energy balls.

4. If desired, roll the energy balls in shredded coconut or cocoa powder for coating.

5. Place the energy balls on a plate or baking sheet lined with parchment paper.

6. Refrigerate the energy balls for at least 30 minutes to firm up.

7. Once chilled, the energy balls are ready to enjoy.

Nutritional Information (per energy ball):

- Calories: 80 kcal

- Carbohydrates: 9g

- Protein: 1.5g

- Fat: 4.5g

- Fiber: 1.5g

Glycemic Value: Low

12.Sugar-Free Pumpkin Pie

Preparation Time: 15 minutes
Cooking Time: 45-50 minutes
Chilling Time: 4 hours
Servings: Makes 8 slices

Ingredients:

For the crust:

- *1 1/2 cups almond flour*
- *1/4 cup coconut oil, melted*
- *1 tablespoon powdered erythritol or sweetener of choice*
- *Pinch of salt*

For the filling:

- *15 ounces canned pumpkin puree*
- *3 large eggs*
- *1/2 cup heavy cream*
- *1/4 cup powdered erythritol or sweetener of choice*
- *1 teaspoon vanilla extract*
- *1 teaspoon ground cinnamon*
- *1/2 teaspoon ground ginger*
- *1/4 teaspoon ground nutmeg*
- *1/4 teaspoon ground cloves*
- *Pinch of salt*

Instructions:

1. Preheat your oven to 350°F (175°C). Grease a 9-inch pie dish with coconut oil or non-stick cooking spray.

2. In a mixing bowl, combine the almond flour, melted coconut oil, powdered erythritol, and a pinch of salt. Mix until well combined and the mixture resembles coarse crumbs.

3. Press the almond flour mixture firmly into the bottom and sides of the greased pie dish to form the crust. Use the back of a spoon or your fingers to press it down evenly.

4. In another mixing bowl, whisk together the canned pumpkin puree, eggs, heavy cream, powdered erythritol, vanilla extract, ground cinnamon, ground ginger, ground nutmeg, ground cloves, and a pinch of salt until smooth and well combined.

5. Pour the pumpkin filling into the prepared pie crust, spreading it out evenly.

6. Bake in the preheated oven for 45-50 minutes, or until the filling is set and the crust is golden brown.

7. Once baked, remove the pie from the oven and let it cool to room temperature.

8. Once cooled, refrigerate the pie for at least 4 hours or overnight to set.

9. Before serving, slice the sugar-free pumpkin pie into 8 slices.

10. Serve chilled and enjoy!

Nutritional Information (per serving - 1 slice):

- Calories: 250 kcal

- Carbohydrates: 9g

- Protein: 6g

- Fat: 21g

- Fiber: 4g

Glycemic Value: Low

13. Raspberry Almond Thumbprint Cookies

Preparation Time: 20 minutes
Cooking Time: 12-15 minutes
Servings: Makes about 20 cookies

Ingredients:

- 1 cup almond flour

- 1/4 cup unsalted butter, softened

- 1/4 cup powdered erythritol or sweetener of choice

- 1 teaspoon almond extract

- 1/4 teaspoon salt

- 1/4 cup sugar-free raspberry jam or preserves

Instructions:

1. Preheat your oven to 350°F (175°C). Line a baking sheet with parchment paper.

2. In a mixing bowl, cream together the softened butter and powdered erythritol until light and fluffy.

3. Add the almond extract and salt to the butter mixture, and mix until well combined.

4. Gradually add the almond flour to the mixture, stirring until a dough forms.

5. Roll the dough into 1-inch balls and place them on the prepared baking sheet, leaving some space between each cookie.

6. Use your thumb or the back of a small spoon to make an indentation in the center of each cookie.

7. Fill each indentation with about 1/2 teaspoon of sugar-free raspberry jam or preserves.

8. Bake in the preheated oven for 12-15 minutes, or until the edges of the cookies are lightly golden.

9. Remove the cookies from the oven and let them cool on the baking sheet for a few minutes.

10. Transfer the cookies to a wire rack to cool completely before serving.

Nutritional Information (per serving - 1 cookie):

- Calories: 70 kcal

- Carbohydrates: 3g

- Protein: 1g

- Fat: 6g

- Fiber: 1g

Glycemic Value: Low

14.No-Bake Peanut Butter Bars

Preparation Time: 15 minutes
Chilling Time: 2 hours
Servings: Makes about 16 bars

Ingredients:

- *1 1/2 cups peanut butter (smooth or crunchy)*

- *1/2 cup honey or maple syrup*

- *1/2 cup coconut oil, melted*

- *2 cups rolled oats*

- *1 cup unsweetened shredded coconut*

- *1 teaspoon vanilla extract*

- *1/4 teaspoon salt*

- *Optional: 1/2 cup dark chocolate chips for drizzling*

Instructions:

1. Line an 8x8 inch baking dish with parchment paper, leaving some overhang on the sides for easy removal of the bars later.

2. In a microwave-safe bowl or on the stovetop, melt the peanut butter, honey or maple syrup, and coconut oil together until smooth and well combined.

3. Stir in the rolled oats, shredded coconut, vanilla extract, and salt until everything is evenly coated.

4. Transfer the mixture into the prepared baking dish and press it down firmly and evenly using the back of a spoon or spatula.

5. If desired, melt the dark chocolate chips in the microwave in 30-second intervals, stirring in between until smooth. Drizzle the melted chocolate over the top of the peanut butter mixture.

6. Place the baking dish in the refrigerator and chill for at least 2 hours, or until the bars are firm and set.

7. Once chilled, use the parchment paper overhang to lift the bars out of the dish. Place them on a cutting board and cut into squares or bars using a sharp knife.

8. Serve the bars immediately, or store them in an airtight container in the refrigerator for up to one week.

Nutritional Information (per serving - 1 bar):

- Calories: 230 kcal

- Carbohydrates: 16g

- Protein: 5g

- Fat: 17g

- Fiber: 2g

Glycemic Value: Moderate

15. Cocoa-Dusted Almonds

Preparation Time: 5 minutes
Cooking Time: 10 minutes
Servings: Makes about 2 cups

Ingredients:

- *2 cups whole almonds*

- *1 tablespoon unsweetened cocoa powder*

- *2 tablespoons powdered erythritol or sweetener of choice*

- *1/2 teaspoon vanilla extract*

- *Pinch of salt*

Instructions:

1. Preheat your oven to 350°F (175°C). Line a baking sheet with parchment paper.

2. In a mixing bowl, combine the almonds, unsweetened cocoa powder, powdered erythritol, vanilla extract, and a pinch of salt. Toss until the almonds are evenly coated.

3. Spread the coated almonds in a single layer on the prepared baking sheet.

4. Bake in the preheated oven for 8-10 minutes, stirring halfway through, until the almonds are toasted and fragrant.

5. Remove the baking sheet from the oven and let the almonds cool completely.

6. Once cooled, transfer the cocoa-dusted almonds to an airtight container for storage.

7. Enjoy as a snack on their own, or sprinkle them over yogurt, oatmeal, or salads for added crunch and flavor.

Nutritional Information (per serving - 1/4 cup):

- Calories: 180 kcal

- Carbohydrates: 6g

- Protein: 7g

- Fat: 15g

- Fiber: 3g

Glycemic Value: Low

Chapter 7: Meal Plan

After successfully completing the first cycle of your 4-week meal plan, extend your meal plan for another 4 weeks by repeating the same recipes and guidelines you've been following so far. This will allow you to consolidate the progress you've made and maintain your structured and balanced diet

Days	Breakfast	Snack	Lunch	Snack	Dinner
1	Greek Yogurt Parfait	Greek Yogurt with Berries	Grilled Chicken Salad with Balsamic Vinaigrette	Cucumber Slices with Hummus	Grilled Salmon with Asparagus
2	Vegetable Omelette	Hard-Boiled Eggs	Quinoa and Vegetable Stir-Fry	Apple Slices with Almond Butter	Turkey Meatballs with Zucchini Noodles
3	Whole Grain Toast with Avocado	Mixed Nuts and Seeds	Turkey and Avocado Wrap	Celery Sticks with Cream Cheese	Baked Chicken Breast with Roasted Vegetables
4	Chia Seed Pudding	Cheese Cubes and Cherry Tomatoes	Salmon and Asparagus Foil Packets	Avocado Slices with Lime and Sea Salt	Quinoa-Stuffed Bell Peppers
5	Banana Nut Oatmeal	Avocado Slices with Lime and Sea Salt	Cauliflower Rice Burrito Bowl	Whole Grain Crackers with Tuna Salad	Stir-Fried Tofu with Broccoli and Brown Rice

6	Spinach and Feta Crustless Quiche	Whole Grain Crackers with Tuna Salad	Lentil Soup with Spinach and Tomatoes	Carrot Sticks with Guacamole	Lemon Herb Roasted Chicken Thighs with Cauliflower Mash
7	Cottage Cheese and Fruit Bowl	Carrot Sticks with Guacamole	Zucchini Noodles with Pesto and Cherry Tomatoes	Edamame Beans	Shrimp Stir-Fry with Snow Peas and Bell Peppers
8	Egg and Vegetable Breakfast Burrito	Edamame Beans	Tofu and Vegetable Stir-Fry with Brown Rice	Sliced Bell Peppers with Cottage Cheese	Eggplant Parmesan with Whole Wheat Pasta
9	Peanut Butter Banana Smoothie	Sliced Bell Peppers with Cottage Cheese	Chickpea Salad with Cucumber and Feta	Turkey Roll-Ups with Lettuce and Mustard	Beef and Vegetable Skewers with Quinoa
10	Turkey Sausage and Veggie Breakfast Casserole	Turkey Roll-Ups with Lettuce and Mustard	Eggplant Parmesan with Whole Wheat	Sugar-Free Jello with Whipped Cream	Mediterranean Chickpea Salad with Grilled Chicken
11	Smoked Salmon and Avocado Toast	Sugar-Free Jello with Whipped Cream	Shrimp and Vegetable Skewers with Quinoa	Homemade Trail Mix	Spinach and Mushroom Stuffed Chicken Breast

12	Berry Protein Smoothie Bowl	Homemade Trail Mix	Greek Salad with Grilled Chicken	Dark Chocolate Avocado Mousse	Blackened Tilapia with Steamed Green Beans
13	Quinoa Breakfast Bowl with Almonds and Berries	Sugar-Free Apple Crisp	Black Bean and Corn Quesadillas	Almond Flour Lemon Cake	Cauliflower Fried Rice with Shrimp
14	Egg Muffins with Spinach and Mushrooms	Sugar-Free Apple Crisp	Spinach and Mushroom Frittata	Chia Seed Pudding with Berries	Greek Turkey Burgers with Greek Salad
15	Low-Carb Breakfast Tacos	Baked Cinnamon Apples	Asian-Inspired Tuna Salad with Sesame Dressing	Coconut Flour Chocolate Chip Cookies	Lentil Soup with Spinach and Tomatoes
16	Greek Yogurt Parfait	Avocado Chocolate Pudding	Grilled Chicken Salad with Balsamic Vinaigrette	Sugar-Free Berry Parfait	Quinoa-Stuffed Bell Peppers
17	Vegetable Omelette	Walnut and Date Energy Balls	Quinoa and Vegetable Stir-Fry	Dark Chocolate Avocado Mousse	Stir-Fried Tofu with Broccoli and Brown Rice

18	Whole Grain Toast with Avocado	Walnut and Date Energy Balls	Turkey and Avocado Wrap	Almond Flour Lemon Cake	Lemon Herb Roasted Chicken Thighs with Cauliflower Mash
19	Chia Seed Pudding	Sugar-Free Pumpkin Pie	Salmon and Asparagus Foil Packets	Chia Seed Pudding with Berries	Shrimp Stir-Fry with Snow Peas and Bell Peppers
20	Banana Nut Oatmeal	Avocado Chocolate Pudding	Cauliflower Rice Burrito Bowl	Homemade Trail Mix	Eggplant Parmesan with Whole Wheat Pasta
21	Spinach and Feta Crustless Quiche	Walnut and Date Energy Balls	Lentil Soup with Spinach and Tomatoes	Sugar-Free Berry Parfait	Beef and Vegetable Skewers with Quinoa
22	Cottage Cheese and Fruit Bowl	Sugar-Free Pumpkin Pie	Zucchini Noodles with Pesto and Cherry Tomatoes	Dark Chocolate Avocado Mousse	Mediterranean Chickpea Salad with Grilled Chicken
23	Egg and Vegetable Breakfast Burrito	Sugar-Free Apple Crisp	Tofu and Vegetable Stir-Fry with Brown Rice	Almond Flour Lemon Cake	Spinach and Mushroom Stuffed Chicken Breast

24	Peanut Butter Banana Smoothie	Baked Cinnamon Apples	Chickpea Salad with Cucumber and Feta	Coconut Flour Chocolate Chip Cookies	Blackened Tilapia with Steamed Green Beans
25	Turkey Sausage and Veggie Breakfast Casserole	Avocado Slices with Lime and Sea Salt	Eggplant Parmesan with Whole Wheat	Sugar-Free Jello with Whipped Cream	Cauliflower Fried Rice with Shrimp
26	Smoked Salmon and Avocado Toast	Whole Grain Crackers with Tuna Salad	Shrimp and Vegetable Skewers with Quinoa	Homemade Trail Mix	Greek Turkey Burgers with Greek Salad
27	Berry Protein Smoothie Bowl	Carrot Sticks with Guacamole	Greek Salad with Grilled Chicken	Cocoa-Dusted Almonds	Lentil Soup with Spinach and Tomatoes
28	Quinoa Breakfast Bowl with Almonds and Berries	Edamame Beans	Black Bean and Corn Quesadillas	Dark Chocolate Avocado Mousse	Quinoa-Stuffed Bell Peppers

Conclusion

Diabetes is a life-threatening disease caused by a lack of insulin. Insulin is a hormone that is required for the body's healthy functioning. The cells in a person's body do not respond to insulin effectively when they acquire diabetes. As a result, the cells do not get the energy and nutrients they require, and they begin to die.

Being diagnosed with diabetes will bring some major changes in your lifestyle. From the time you are diagnosed with it, it would always be a constant battle with food. You need to become a lot more careful with your food choices and the quantity that you eat. Every meal will feel like a major effort. You will be planning every day for the whole week, well in advance. Depending upon the type of food you ate, you have to keep checking your blood sugar levels. You may get used to taking long breaks between meals and staying away from snacks between dinner and breakfast.

Food would be treated as a bomb like it can go off at any time. According to an old saying, "When the body gets too hot, then your body heads straight to the kitchen."

Managing diabetes can be a very, very stressful ordeal. There will be many times that you will mark your glucose levels down on a piece of paper like you are plotting graph lines or something. You will mix your insulin shots up and then stress about whether or not you are giving yourself the right dosage. You will always be over-cautious because it involves a LOT of math and a really fine margin of error. But now, those days are gone!

With the help of technology and books, you can stock your kitchen with the right foods, like meal plans, diabetic friendly dishes, etc. You can also get an app that will even do the work for you. You can also people-watch on the internet and find the know-how to cook and eat right; you will always be a few meals away from certain disasters, like a plummeting blood sugar level. Always carry some sugar in your pocket. You won't have to experience the pangs of hunger but if you are unlucky, you will have to ration your food and bring along some simple low-calorie snacks with you.

This is the future of diabetes.

As you've reached the end of this book, you have gained complete control of your diabetes and this is where your expedition towards a better, healthier life starts. I hope I was able to inculcate some knowledge into you and make this adventure a little bit less of a struggle.

I would like to remind you that you're not alone in having to manage this disease and that nearly 85% of the new cases are 20 years old or younger.

Regardless of the length or seriousness of your diabetes, it can be managed! Take the information presented here and start with it!

Preparation is key to having a healthier and happier life.

It's helpful to remember that every tool at your disposal can help in some way.

Thank you for choosing our book **"Diabetic Cookbook for Beginners."**

We greatly appreciate your support and are excited to offer you a special bonus as a token of our gratitude.

Bonus: "Diabetic Dessert Cookbook Bonus Edition"

To access your exclusive bonus, we invite you to scan the QR code below using the camera on your smartphone or tablet. This will take you directly to the download page for our additional eBook, which contains 60 delicious bonus recipes to satisfy your sweet cravings in a healthy and tasty way.

We can't wait for you to try out these delightful recipes and enjoy their unique flavors. Thank you again for choosing our book and for your continued support.

Happy cooking!

Best regards,

Nathan Terrell

Printed in Great Britain
by Amazon

42370240R00064